HERMÈS

Publicis EtNous

marset

Dipping Light by Jordi Canudas
Taking care of light

Curious
Alchemy

An innovation in paper science for 2018

arjowigginscreativepapers.com
Distributed by Antalis

PARACHUTE

The calm before the calm.

PARACHUTEHOME.COM

OUUR

KINFOLK

FOUNDER & CREATIVE DIRECTOR
Nathan Williams

EDITOR-IN-CHIEF
Julie Cirelli

EDITOR
John Clifford Burns

DEPUTY EDITOR
Harriet Fitch Little

ART DIRECTOR
Christian Møller Andersen

DESIGN DIRECTOR
Alex Hunting

BRAND DIRECTOR
Amy Woodroffe

COPY EDITOR
Rachel Holzman

COMMUNICATIONS DIRECTOR
Jessica Gray

PRODUCER
Cecilie Jegsen

CASTING DIRECTOR
Sarah Bunter

**SALES & DISTRIBUTION
DIRECTOR**
Frédéric Mähl

**BUSINESS OPERATIONS
MANAGER**
Kasper Schademan

STUDIO MANAGER
Aryana Tajdivand-Echevarria

EDITORIAL ASSISTANTS
Oliver Hugemark
Ulrika Lukševica
Garett Nelson

SALES ASSISTANT
Jonas Steen Andersen

CONTRIBUTING EDITORS
Michael Anastassiades
Jonas Bjerre-Poulsen
Andrea Codrington Lippke
Ilse Crawford
Margot Henderson
Leonard Koren
Hans Ulrich Obrist
Amy Sall
Matt Willey

STYLING, HAIR & MAKEUP
Sue Choi
Ashleigh Ciucci
Louis Philippe de Gagoue
Antonio De Luca
Kirstine Engell
Andreas Frienholt
Barbara Gullstein
Debbie Hsieh
Lovisa Lunneborg
Teddy Mitchell
David Nolan
Nicque Patterson
Carolyne Rapp
Stine Rasmussen

CROSSWORD
Molly Young

PUBLICATION DESIGN
Alex Hunting Studio

COVER PHOTOGRAPHY
Pelle Crépin

WORDS
Alex Anderson
Ellie Violet Bramley
Matt Castle
Alia Gilbert
Pamela K. Johnson
Daniel Mallory Ortberg
Kyla Marshell
Sarah Moroz
John Ovans
Sala Elise Patterson
Lydia Pyne
Debika Ray
Asher Ross
Tristan Rutherford
Laura Rysman
Neda Semnani
Charles Shafaieh
Pip Usher

PHOTOGRAPHY
Gustav Almestål
Barbara Pym Society
Pelle Crépin
Mark Draisey
Christopher Ferguson
Lasse Fløde
Suzanne Fournier-Schlegel
Philippe Fragniere
Jean-Marie Franceschi
Cecilie Jegsen
Paul Jung
Billy Kidd
Paul Kremer
Salva López
Panos Lyris
Oscar Meyer
Emman Montalvan
Melvin Sokolsky
Marsý Hild Þórsdóttir
Aaron Tilley
Zoltan Tombor
Cédric Viollet

ISSUE 29

info@kinfolk.com
www.kinfolk.com

Published by Ouur Media
Amagertorv 14, Level 1
1160 Copenhagen, Denmark

The views expressed in Kinfolk magazine are those of the respective contributors and are not necessarily shared by the company or its staff.

SUBSCRIBE
Kinfolk is published four times a year. To subscribe, visit kinfolk.com/subscribe or email us at info@kinfolk.com

CONTACT US
If you have questions or comments, please write to us at info@kinfolk.com. For advertising inquiries, get in touch at advertising@kinfolk.com

danish design by · made by LINDBERG

håndværk

A specialist label creating *luxury basics*.
Ethically crafted with an unwavering
commitment to *exceptional quality*.

handvaerk.com

Issue 29

Welcome

"The page that was blank to begin with is now crossed from top to bottom with tiny black characters—letters, words, commas, exclamation marks—and it's because of them the page is said to be legible," begins Jean Genet's *Prisoner of Love,* a memoir of his encounters with Palestinian fighters and Black Panthers during the 1970s. He continues: "But a kind of uneasiness, a feeling close to nausea, an irresolution that stays my hand—these make me wonder: do these black marks add up to reality?"

Concerns over fake news and press freedom have usurped a media dilemma over whether or not print is dead (it's not) with an altogether more existential thought: To what extent can words reflect reality? Did Genet, a Frenchman, achieve a true representation of the Palestinian or African-American experience in *Prisoner of Love*? Do today's newspapers, for that matter?

Putting pen to paper is a powerful act: What we write and read shapes the way that we—and others—think about the world and each other. Journalism changes society; literature changes lives. This issue of *Kinfolk* celebrates the power of print, from the tactile pleasures of its material parts to the potency of the written word. In New York, Charles Shafaieh meets author André Aciman, who offers a spot of advice for modern readers: "Paper will automatically want to create order, symmetry, harmony and meaning. You have to distrust that."

Elsewhere, Parisian calligrapher Nicolas Ouchenir sheds light on the lost art of handwriting; author Lydia Pyne reveals the secret lives of bookshelves; writer Neda Semnani dissects how the passport—a seemingly simple document of "a few dozen pages between a laminated cardboard cover"—has become the most important piece of paper one can ever possess; and we explore the numerous other ways in which printed matter stills matters—from mail to money, and from magazines to memory.

Also in this issue, writer Pamela K. Johnson charts the transition of the self-care movement from its radical margins to the mass-market mainstream, and we meet Anh Duong—an actress and artist for whom painting is an opportunity to express "the inside suffering" so seldom projected otherwise. We also meet seminal Iranian photographer Shirin Neshat and explore the home of the late Catalan sculptor Xavier Corberó, whose labyrinthine estate is as kaleidoscopic as the stories—on pepper, lip-syncing, lullabies, personal space—in this issue.

JOHN CLIFFORD BURNS

"The outcome of what I do has to be poetry."
XAVIER CORBERÓ – P. 54

OVO – The perfect balance

Ovo is a refined easy chair, designed by Damian Williamson, with striking curves resting on a rigid squared steel frame. The same steel is also used as a beautiful slim line connecting the back and the front of the chair. As a result, you achieve a playful integration between the leather and the steel while hiding the stitched seam at the same time.

The Ovo design is first and foremost about generosity but also great comfort. The chair is welcoming and very comfortable to sit in – it invites you to sit back and relax. Whether you place it in the comfort of your own private home, a relaxing hotel suite or a lobby, it will be the perfect fit.

"A page of literature doesn't beat good company."
ANDRÉ ACIMAN — P. 134

Photograph: Pelle Crépin

ARTFUL CONSTRUCTION. ELEVATED DETAILS. LEVI'S® BY DESIGN.

Featuring Lily Aldridge

RAINS

Drip, drip, drip.

rains.com

1
Starters

ALEX ANDERSON

In Praise of Cliché

Don't cry over spilled milk. Every aphorism has a silver lining.

Mechanically reproduced thought: how handy! Such must have been the musings of the French typesetters who coined *cliché* in the early 19th century, initially as a word to describe the cast plates that printers used to more quickly reproduce common images and phrases.

What's done is done, and there's no use crying over spilled milk, but perhaps they should have given the word a more grating, fingernail-on-chalkboard quality—which clichés often deliver. "An intellectual disgrace," James Parker of *The Boston Globe* calls them, reserving his full contempt for the politicians who are "almost obliged to speak in cliché for fear they will stray into that zone most terrifying to the electorate—the heady unpredictable zone of original thought." Other experts slew the blame toward professional writers. "Of all genres," declares philologist Orin Hargraves, "none is more cliché-burdened today than journalism." From these lamentable sources the problem spreads, virus-like, through incautious listeners. Hargraves complains that they become "unwitting vectors of these forms of words when they write and speak." Stock phrases are everywhere and hard to eradicate.

But why such ire about clichés? A cliché is, by the Oxford English Dictionary's authoritative definition, "a stereotyped expression, a commonplace phrase." However, we have come to understand it as something more dreadful than this definition suggests: an overused idea, often quite clever originally, that has lost its shine, even lost its meaning, from excessive wear and misapplication. It no longer cuts the mustard (or is that cuts muster?). Clichés are annoying, but it is difficult to explain why they bother us. To do this, it helps to look beyond words.

The idea of cliché has expanded past speech and writing into film, painting, music, fashion, design—anywhere creative thinking holds sway. In these domains, using a cliché—the stock plot, the same old riff, the reused detail—replaces the hard effort of new thought with imitation and repetition. We have come to allow that this is somehow flattering to the imitated, but we really see it as a symptom of laziness. Incautious repetition can also be corrosive to the work. American philosopher Albert Borgmann explains in *Technology and the Character of Contemporary Life* that as works of art lose uniqueness, they also lose their "focusing power." They are no longer "clear and articulate," and they cease to "center and illuminate our lives." The blurred contours of repeated ideas and words allow our interest to slip away.

Not every cliché deadens thought, though. Cubist and dada artists of the early 20th century, and pop artists a few decades later, famously turned cliché to their own creative ends. They appropriated hackneyed ideas, phrases and images and reassembled and recharged them, often ironically, in their powerful collages, poems and lithographs. These artists emphasized that commonplace ideas underlie the collective consciousness and bind a culture together. The artists' ironic use of clichés also cryptically reinforced bonds with collaborators; cliché became their inside joke.

Clichés can function similarly in more common usage, when our responsibilities to culture are not especially solemn. A recent champion of these idioms, essayist and critic Hephzibah Anderson, points out that clichés can connect us and help us communicate with others. We often repeat them intentionally—not out of laziness—but because we know from experience that a standard line will carry meaning precisely and with comfortable familiarity. A well-worn witty phrase, judiciously tossed into conversation or prose, can still add a little fun.

Our language and our forms of communication aren't stuck in time: New clichés are always creeping into the culture. And the omnipresent emoji is today's digital analogue to the printers' cast plates of days gone by. It clicks easily into our most casual writing and, like a time-honored cliché, it conveys shared feeling almost effortlessly. Electronically reproduced emotion: how handy.

ELLIE VIOLET BRAMLEY

Word: Adulting

A call to embrace your age, not perform it.

Etymology: In the '80s, "adulting" was used, according to Merriam-Webster, "as a jocular verbal form of the noun adultery." By the late aughties, Twitter users had begun to use it in its current incarnation—to describe adults doing the quotidian tasks that adults are expected to do.

Meaning: Although adulting has appeared on social media since 2008, it arguably entered the mainstream through the work of American writer Kelly Williams Brown and her book *Adulting: How to Become a Grown-up in 468 Easy(ish) Steps*. In 2014, it was added to the Urban Dictionary and has been popping up with increasing frequency, employed by brands including AmEx and Amazon, ever since.

Fortunately, adulting has stayed largely online. Rarely spoken, it often appears in tweets such as: "Adulting is having your day ruined because you couldn't find your Tupperware" or, simply, "adulting is hard." As a hashtag, it follows remarks about doing laundry or cooking pasta, or—with irony—an admission of having cake for breakfast.

This depiction of adulthood as a performative state—a thing to do rather than be, but never for long before boomeranging back to suspended adolescence—has been read as a device for millennials to laud their status as adults while simultaneously distancing themselves from it. But this mix of self-aggrandizement and self-deprecation plays into the hands of those set on millennial-bashing; this "lost generation" can't even pay their taxes without Snapchatting about it.

There's a gender dimension, too. It is used more often than not by young women, employed in a way that has been described as "self-referentially ironic." But in feeding a Pinterest vision of adulthood that's cutesy and twee—"I'm done adulting. Let's be mermaids," declares one cloying meme—it opens the door to the belittlement of women, millennials or—jackpot—millennial women. It is, wrote one *Washington Post* journalist last year, "a self-infantilizing rejection of female maturity in a culture that already has almost no love for grown-up women."

We are living in an era where many of the traditional markers of maturing are being impeded—inflated house prices and an insecure job market conspire to keep young adults young. Writing in *The Lancet* recently, scientists declared that adolescence, which used to end abruptly at 19, now extends to 24. As such, the concept of "adulting," though irritating, becomes a sometimes sad, sometimes cathartically funny reminder of the often enforced stunting of a generation's growth.

GOOD ON PAPER
by Harriet Fitch Little

The savvy visitor knows that no stay in Japan is complete without a trip to the drugstore to stock up on skincare products. But in recent years, a new pilgrimage has gained prominence: a visit to the stationery store. *Techo* culture is just the most recent iteration of a national fascination with pens, paper and planners: A tradition of calligraphy has given rise to a thriving trade in precision ballpoints; an illustrious history of origami has morphed into a market for craft paper in every hue. Designs are dominated by the *kawaii* ethos—an appreciation for all things cute—yet consumers remain rigorous critics of novelty products not built to last. (Top: Envelopes by Original Crown Mill, Center: Scissors by Craft Design Technology, Bottom: Brass pen case by Traveler's Company.)

Left Photograph: Panos Lyris, Right Photographs: Christian Møller Andersen

A short history of the corridor.

CHARLES SHAFAIEH

Passage of Time

The brute efficiency that made corridors so popular among modern architects is now responsible for them falling out of favor; they are perceived to be too institutional.

Corridors—transitional, purely functional spaces—seem a ubiquitous architectural feature in offices, subway systems and many homes. This, however, was not always the case.

The word derives from the Spanish *corredor* (runner), messengers in 14th-century Spain for whom nobles built passageways that would expedite their journeys. Elsewhere in Europe, in palaces like Versailles or large public buildings, rooms were not connected to or separated from each other with corridors. Rather, they were designed as *enfilades*—suites in which one room led directly into another.

Enfilade's second meaning—in combat, being attacked from the vulnerable, more exposed flank position—is a fitting metaphor for the classist obsession with corridors in 19th-century Britain. "In country homes, there was a fixation with dividing the family corridor from the servants' and visitors'," says professor Roger Luckhurst, author of the forthcoming book *The Corridor*. "Corridors would disguise you from being seen, which obsessed, for example, the fifth Duke of Portland, who built 10 miles of corridors underneath his house."

Yet corridors have brought people together too, as in utopian socialist projects like Charles Fourier's sexually radical *phalanstères*. These massive buildings, meant to house about 1,600 people, were to feature a covered, heated corridor extending along their first story. Luckhurst notes that in phalanstères "the entire community lived along what Fourier called a 'street gallery,' so that everyone could have sex as quickly as possible"—not unlike college dormitories. The Soviet Union also used a unifying corridor in their *kommunalka* apartments, in which strangers and family alike were connected by an open space that led to tiny private bedrooms and otherwise communal spaces.

Today, however, many corridors are disappearing as office architects deem them claustrophobic emblems of bureaucracy. Instead, they favor open-plan spaces, which paradoxically limit the chance encounters between people from different disciplines. It may be true that corridors can engender discomfort, even dread—consider their presence in horror movies like *The Shining*—but never knowing what their doors may reveal or who will emerge from them can be productive, too. David Lynch, whose films contain many enigmatic passageways, believes so. "Secrets and mysteries provide a beautiful corridor where you can float out," he muses. "I love the process of going into mystery."

Photograph: Cecilie Jegsen

JOHN OVANS

Mime Culture

On lip-syncing and the allure of mouthing along.

Photograph: Tooker Lips by Melvin Sokolsky, 1961

Lip-syncing was once banned in Turkmenistan. In 2005, the country's then-dictator, Saparmurat Niyazov, cited its "negative effect on the development of singing and musical art" and outlawed it (along with gold teeth, ballet and beards).

Niyazov was fighting a losing battle: 2005 was an auspicious year for lip-syncing, arguably the moment at which this form of cultural expression ascended to the mainstream. It was the year that Google acquired YouTube after its CEO was won over by a grainy homemade video of two Chinese students passionately mouthing along to *I Want It That Way* by the Backstreet Boys. They had recorded the video on a webcam in their university dorm room and then uploaded it to YouTube. Viewers were gripped—watching it by the thousands and sending in requests begging for more.

Come 2018, lip-syncing's cultural ubiquity is uncontested, thanks to apps such as Dubsmash and Musical.ly, which have bred a whole generation of non-singing singers. What was once a very private pastime—you, a hairbrush, and your own reflection—has gone digital. Yet the essence of its appeal remains the same: It seems there's no better way to express yourself than by borrowing somebody else's voice.

Lip-syncing owes much of its position as a pop culture phenomenon today to the underground ballroom drag scene of 1980s New York, famously captured at its peak in the documentary *Paris Is Burning*. Balls were pageant-style events frequented by predominately queer people of color who would compete, or "walk," in categories such as dance, costumes, voguing and lip-syncing, often with the aim to satirize masculinity or femininity through appearance. The balls were safe havens for gender expression, where "playing at being" represented a form of liberation for marginalized communities. Lip-syncing was a chance for gay men and trans women to "steal" a voice from a female celebrity—often a troubled diva or Hollywood actress whose pain they felt affinity with, and whose sexuality and glamour they could channel.

Lip-syncing has remained the bread and butter of drag performers in the decades since, exported from smoky bars and ballrooms onto television thanks to its central role on *RuPaul's Drag Race*. The craze shows no sign of dying down—it seems we all want to emulate our idols. "It's really just people looking for a richer way to express what they actually feel at the moment," Dubsmash's founder, Suchit Dash, told *The New York Times* after the app's release. In the age of information overload, lip-syncing has evolved from an act of self-expression to one of communication, often allowing us to verbalize (with the multi-octave range of Mariah) what might normally be forbidden. We all have a secret life to share—and now our audience can be bigger than our reflection in the mirror.

For drag performers in 1980s New York, the artifice of singing in a voice other than their own became an expression of authenticity.

STARTERS

Photograph: Cédric Viollet, Styling: Louis Philippe de Gagoue

A stylist with a big wardrobe becomes a photographer with an even bigger vision.

JOHN CLIFFORD BURNS

Louis Philippe de Gagoue

Last summer, Louis Philippe de Gagoue photographed a male model as he lay in a pile of trash wearing nothing but a red Speedo, a tin foil hat and some Post-it notes. It was a personal project, but the effect was similar to a cover he shot for *Vogue Netherlands* a season prior (except then the model wore Miu Miu): excessive and glamorous, yet without glossy pretension. In just a few years, de Gagoue has transitioned from model to stylist, from blogger to signed fashion photographer. What drives his success, he says, is what also allows him to stroll around Paris wearing a tuxedo jacket and a pair of rubber gloves: confidence.

You initially gained a following through your personal style, but you've now shot for major titles including several countries' editions of *Vogue*. Are you enjoying yourself? Yes, I'm so happy. When I started out, I was using an analog camera and didn't know anything about the settings. It was a joke. But I've now been chosen by *Vogue Italia* as a finalist for a photography prize and I've had an exhibition in Milan and signed to an agency in Paris.

You seem to be traveling constantly. Where do you feel most at home? I'm from Ivory Coast, live between Cameroon and Paris, and spend a lot of time in Morocco. I can't stay in one place and I don't like routine. I need to travel.

Were any skills you learned at law school transferable to the fashion industry? Everyone in my family went to law school, so I decided to go too. The only important thing I learned there was to be confident. You can get away with murder.

Is your work ever political? Politics is not my cup of tea, but I do try to communicate a different view of Africa. And I prefer to shoot models who look powerful rather than beautiful. Beauty comes from attitude, not appearance.

How long do you see yourself doing this? I'm obsessed with photographs and could never stop taking them. So, until I lose my vision or get really old.

What's the most boring scenario imaginable for you? I hate to compromise. As a stylist, you work with different photographers and often don't have the same vision. Now I do both, I don't have restrictions; no one can tell me to do this or that. I think my work is more powerful as a result.

GUESSING GAMES

by Harriet Fitch Little

Political experts are terrible at predicting actual political outcomes. According to research done at the University of Pennsylvania, they are only marginally better at it than "dart-throwing chimps." But what's the alternative? According to Philip Tetlock and Dan Gardner, authors of *Superforecasting: The Art & Science of Prediction*, we should look to the "super predictors"—ordinary people who they have identified through mass testing as performing four times better than average at anticipating major world events. The super predictors aren't political insiders— one standout participant was a pharmacist—but what they do have in common is self-awareness and open-mindedness. It seems that sometimes the pros are so certain of where the ball will land that they neglect to watch its flight. However, there is a curious logic to support the contention that stubborn self-confidence is the pathway to success—at least, in sports. In 2015, Swedish researchers Olof Rosenqvist and Oskar Nordstrom Skans studied the performance outcomes of golfers of almost identical ability, the only difference being that half had made the cut for an important tournament and the other half had narrowly missed out. Despite the hairline difference in ability between the two groups, researchers found that those who gained entry to the tournament went on to perform better in future games than those who didn't. The conclusion? Perhaps athletes aren't so foolish to work on the presumption that old patterns will predict future performance: As the saying goes, nothing succeeds like success. *Photography by Mark Draisey.*

Malene Bach

The Danish artist discusses how to use color intelligently at home.

Photograph: Oscar Meyer

Malene Bach creates symphonies of color. She uses paint in audacious but measured doses, in meaningful places and studied hues. The effect is thrilling.

Bach's portfolio reflects an eclectic career dominated by a sense of fun: She has painted on canvas and grainy wood, but also masterminded a contemporary reinterpretation of a Romanesque church, outdoor sculptures, an indoor swimming pool, installations, ornamentation and videos. Her work is deceptively simple: What you see are bold shapes and pigment, but what you feel is energy.

You work in so many mediums. Which was your starting point? My father is a painter, so I've been working with paint since I was a kid. But after my studies, I started to get more interested in the relationship between color and space. I worked more and more in three-dimensional spaces, still with paint but using it as a material—as a form with volume. This process took me away from the canvas. We call it painting in the extended field, or painting beyond the frame.

How do you think about color? Color never stands alone. When I think about how color meets the space, I consider how much space it takes up and where in the space it's situated. Material is also a part of it: If you have a yellow raincoat or a yellow carpet or a pane of transparent yellow glass, then the yellow looks different in every context.

Even the same shade of yellow? Exactly. So, this is why yellow is not only yellow. It's always related to something else, always bound in a material.

Is there a common mistake people make when adding color to their homes? Often people say, "Oh, we should add some color," so they'll paint the walls red or blue. But what happens then is that all other colors in the space are rejected. I always work with colors in which all other colors would feel good. I learned a trick from Le Corbusier, the architect. If you have a blue and want to make it grayer, the way they do it today is by adding white and black. The right way to make a color grayer would be to add its contrasting color.

Do you dislike white walls? Oh no. Sometimes you just need white because maybe you have a lot of nice colorful objects in the space. But do you know what I think is a nightmare? When you walk into these big companies and everything is white, black and gray. This is tyranny. It's like brainwashing. What color does is actually connect people to a space, to a place. When there's color, it welcomes senses, feelings, happiness, sorrow, laughter, lust, dreams, memories. If there's no color at all, there's no space to be a human being.

How do you approach site-specific work? I always work within the context. How deep can you dig into the history of a place, the site, the geography of the building itself? This is very important because this is part of the identity of a space.

What do you wish for people who interact with something you've created? When people suddenly realize what they are sensing, that's enough for me. The present moment becomes totally clear and you feel alive. It's very life-affirming.

DEBIKA RAY

How to Hold a Grudge

In defense of a petty pleasure.

How glorious it feels to hold a grudge. How satisfying and self-indulgent. A true grudge is not about bitterness, hatred, vengeance or anger. Nor is it a feeling that demands action or a solution. Rather, it is the smug pleasure of knowing that you're entitled to feel wronged—a privately held insight into another person's flaws. It is also, importantly, an emotional shield—a slight lowering of expectations that immunizes you against being disappointed again.

According to author Sophie Hannah, holding personal grudges can be constructive. In November, she is launching a self-help book dashing the conventional wisdom that grudges are unhealthy, and that functional people always "forgive and forget." *How to Hold a Grudge: From Resentment to Contentment, the Power of Grudges to Transform Your Life* includes an "anthology of grudges"—such as a man who stood in line for hours in the rain to see a James Bond film for which tickets had sold out, and then went on to boycott the franchise forever.

Hannah claims that if we hold grudges "responsibly," they can offer us a lesson and help us to be more forgiving. "It's a way of honoring your negative experiences. If you stop trying to resist and let yourself feel, you can take action to protect yourself in future and move on without feeling there was an injustice that should have been paid attention to." Analyzing the kinds of grudges you hold, she says, can also be a useful way to understand your own value system.

Not every grudge has the potential to be edifying, however, particularly when the stakes are high. The rivalry between inventors Thomas Edison and Nikola Tesla may have delayed the arrival of electricity in our homes by half a century. Artist Paul Gauguin's aversion to Vincent Van Gogh is believed to have contributed to the latter cutting off his own ear. And, at the petty end of the celebrity spectrum, author J.K. Rowling was allegedly so stung by a patronizing comment by Stephen Fry that she inserted a phrase he had difficulty pronouncing into every subsequent Harry Potter book, to trip him up when he was narrating the audio version of the series.

Others have tried to use grudges to their advantage. In the 2014 book *HRC*, for example, political journalists Jonathan Allen and Amie Parnes claimed that Hillary and Bill Clinton had drawn up a list of people who had pleased or displeased them during Hillary's 2008 run for the Democratic presidential nomination. Complete with rankings to indicate the strength of their good deed or the severity of their infraction, the spreadsheet was presumably a guide to who should be rewarded or punished, relied upon or mistrusted, as Hillary continued her political career. How history has since played out is perhaps a warning that grudges, no matter how numerous or neatly filed, are not necessarily a path to power.

Sports fans often define themselves as a group by holding communal grudges against other teams. The "grudge match"—a competition between two long-term rivals teams —is a calendar highlight.

Phillip K. Smith III

How public art can create community and prompt personal reflection.

Phillip K. Smith III thinks he's doing a good job. He believes humans desire love, connection and beauty; if his art can take care of two out of the three—beauty and community—then he is satisfied. An artist whose primary medium is light, Smith installs lonesome installations within the desolate landscapes surrounding his native Palm Springs, often using mirrors to reflect the Californian sun as it bathes the red and yellow rock in sunlight and shadow. Here, in collaboration with COS, Smith discusses his most recent commission, *Open Sky*, which transplanted his approach into the fray of Milan's Salone del Mobile. In this piece, his mirror structure draws the Italian sky down into the courtyard of a 16th-century palazzo.

In what ways can public art foster a sense of community? There's a desire for humans to feel connected. We should certainly celebrate our differences, but it's more powerful to celebrate what we have in common—the things that unite us. That's the power of the *Open Sky* project at Salone del Mobile—it focuses the eye on the sky, which connects all of us—no matter where we live.

Your work plays with the law of reflection. Do you also use mirrors to encourage philosophical reflection? Reflecting the landscape through mirrors allows viewers to slow down. It's a place and an opportunity to step away from your schedule, current priorities, pressures or whatever is irritating your mind. It gives you a moment to step back and reconsider—hear every single sound of nature, listen to the wind. Everything washes away and you begin to align and connect yourself with the pace of the work.

Open Sky was commissioned by COS. How do you feel about blurring the lines between art and fashion? Commercialism and the art world are almost always not friends. But I'd say that there's been no difference between working with COS and with a museum that has called me up to say, "We love your work. We have this space, a budget, and we'd like to work with you." COS expressed to me from the beginning that they wanted to support me as an artist. It gives them an opportunity to think about their work through new eyes, and it gives me an opportunity to think about my own, too. I have total respect for that. It's how all creatives should work—without blinders.

How important is human experience in your exhibitions? Trying to craft a relationship between the viewer and the work is important to me. It grew out of going to galleries in New York when I was a freshman at university and realizing that looking at art is a bit like opening somebody's diary but not knowing what happened before or after. There's no connection. I think scale and the procession through the work is important for all of that. *The Circle of Land and Sky* [an installation in Palm Desert] could handle one person, 10 people, 150 people, and it still felt like it was somehow intimate, like there was a sense of shelter.

Do you ever become blind to the beauty of the Palm Springs landscape? Whenever I left my old studio in Indio, I would be on the freeway headed toward Los Angeles and all I would see was the sunset, every single day for about 14 years. That starts to affect you, in a positive way. I started to think about how I could get that perfect gradient, that color, in my work. And so, I look at the landscape as source material for what I'm working on daily. No matter where I travel, I really enjoy coming back to the desert. It's part of my blood, it's part of who I am and I know it and love it. I've lived here for most of my life, but it's still fresh inspiration for me every day.

—

This feature is produced in partnership with COS.

"We should certainly celebrate our differences, but it's more powerful to celebrate what we have in common."

Pep Talk

Does pepper deserve its seat at the table?

Humans need salt to survive. It's our chief source of both sodium and chloride, essential substances that our bodies cannot produce on their own. Depending on where we live, we sprinkle it on by hand, bake foods inside of it, and drizzle it over dishes in liquid forms like soy or fish sauce. It's also an indispensable ingredient in food preservation.

By contrast, *Piper nigrum*, the black pepper that enjoys pride of place alongside salt on most Western tables, is a luxury of subjective value. In the flavor-starved Europe of the middle ages, black pepper—native to south India—commanded obscene prices, to the point that it was sometimes used as a currency in itself. Chefs for noble families heaped it on in proportions we would now find alarming.

Pepper's scarcity imbued it with a deep allure. Western fantasists imagined faraway kingdoms of preposterous wealth founded on pepper and other spices. The reality was far less poetic. Europeans introduced to the ancient spice routes a determination to control foreign means of production. Port cities like Malacca in Malaysia, long the site of wondrous cosmopolitan blending,

came under European control by outright brutality. As Voltaire once wrote, there was no pepper enjoyed in Europe that was not "dyed red with blood."

Centuries of violence and desire lie forgotten in the humble peppercorn, which now can be found everywhere—usually stale. Lior Lev Sercarz, who provides spice blends to Michelin-starred chefs and private individuals as proprietor of New York's La Boîte, has made it his life's work to break the reliance on repetitive spicing. "I often joke when I do classes or talks that hopefully one day every recipe won't end with 'season to taste with salt and pepper,'" he says, "but rather 'season to taste with salinity and heat.'"

Sercarz is not short on alternatives: "Chiles, obviously, but also ginger, horseradish or Szechuan peppercorns. Also the Japanese *sansho* pepper, which is not really a pepper at all, but a berry."

Black pepper is habitual, comforting and ubiquitous. But we owe it to ourselves—and to the memory of the flavor-starved medieval gourmands—to taste something new. As Sercarz says, "One salt shaker and one pepper mill are not the complete truth."

PEPPER MILLS

by Harriet Fitch Little

The restaurant pepper mill is ubiquitous, yet anomalous: Waiters don't season dishes with cumin or chopped cilantro tableside—why pepper? The answer: For tips. Prior to the 20th century, serving staff could make an impression by plating food at the table. When dining out filtered down to become an indulgence of the middle class, corners had to be cut. Pepper, while not particularly well-suited to being a last-minute addition, still had a certain culinary cachet and was retained as a nod to the glory days of personalized service. In turn, the design of the pepper mill became increasingly ostentatious—its body often as long as a waiter's arm, its twist-and-crunch as loud as stepping on a freshly gravelled path. (Top: Large Salt/Pepper Mill by Lostine, Center: Italic Pepper Mill by Carl Auböck, Bottom: MP0210 Pepper Mill by Ettore Sottsass for Alessi.)

Left Photograph: Florilegius/SSPL/Getty Images, Right Photographs: See Credits on page 191

ELLIE VIOLET BRAMLEY

Lost in Space

Technology is inflating our personal bubbles. Should we pop them?

Every time we interact, our personal space is being negotiated. It is a subtle and intuitive dance that only becomes conscious when someone puts a foot wrong and leans in too close, smells too strongly, speaks too loudly. We generally measure the size of our private bubble in terms of physical proximity. But today, technology is rewriting these complicated dance steps in another sphere: It's not where we stand but what we *hear* when we are in close proximity that is changing.

Personal space is at the heart of how we communicate with one another, and how we define it has society-wide ramifications. It has been described by neuroscientist Michael Graziano as a "second skin"—a spatial scaffold that affects our interactions. Yet there has been relatively little interrogation of how technology is reconfiguring that scaffolding.

Last year, musician Damon Krukowski made *Ways of Hearing,* a podcast that looked at sound and personal space. The single most important purchase of his adolescence was a stereo. With it he could fill his bedroom with sound—a sign, he says, that this was his space. Now all it takes is headphones. We are avoiding "ear contact," Krukowski thinks.

It's unclear what came first: Is technology moving us away from one another? Or is it simply meeting a human requirement for personal space? We've always had the need, but we are increasingly struggling to meet it. A recent study found that the concept of personal space is even maintained by human beings in virtual reality situations. This suggests that it would be unfair to paint technology as the black-and-white villain, or at least that the picture is blurry.

Technology can provide a psychological pressure valve, a buffer against the physical invasion of personal space many of us experience every day. "The more we consider ourselves in our personal space," says Krukowski, "I think by definition the less we are engaged in social space." Perhaps it's a shift we should examine rather than sleepwalk into. "We have to be careful where we want to be on that spectrum."

Photograph: Paul Jung/The Licensing Project

Unpicking our obsession with originality.

CHARLES SHAFAIEH

On Copycats

What counts as "authentic" varies enormously between cultures. Japan's Ise Grand Shrine has been removed from Unesco's World Heritage list because it is rebuilt from scratch every 20 years.

How much less valuable is a copy than an original work of art? Consider *Salvator Mundi*, the painting that went to auction at Christie's in November 2017. In 2005, when it was thought to be one of multiple copies of a lost Leonardo da Vinci work, it sold for just $10,000. Then a group of art historians caused controversy by declaring that the Florentine master had himself painted it.

Among them was Martin Kemp, who commented that the work possesses an "uncanny presence" similar to other da Vincis—funny, considering that this quality is, by definition, difficult to pin down.

Even more complicated was the fact that extensive restoration had been undertaken to improve upon its cracked canvas and layers of overpainting, meaning that—whatever its origins—the work had undoubtedly been touched by multiple hands. But da Vinci's name alone spurred Abu Dhabi to spend a record-breaking $450 million on the painting—a move designed to lend cultural cachet to, and boost tourism for, its new "copy" of Paris' Louvre.

Outside the realm of market value though, "the original" is a strange, problematic and even nonsensical concept. As philosopher Jacques Derrida insisted, the very existence of an "original" presupposes the existence of "repetition." And in his 1936 essay, *The Work of Art in the Age of Mechanical Reproduction*, cultural critic Walter Benjamin remarked that in the 20th century, art even becomes "designed for reproducibility."

For the Asante carvers in Ghana, reproducibility has positive connotations. Professor of art history Sidney Littlefield Kasfir observes that, to them, "imitating a well-known model is considered neither deceptive nor demanding; rather it is viewed as both economically pragmatic and a way of legitimating the skill of a predecessor... or paying homage to a fellow artist."

In Chinese art, a masterwork of painting may never be finished. Philosopher Byung-Chul Han notes that, contrary to European practices, such art is "subject to continual change and permanent transcription" as new owners apply their personal seals and other forms of inscription to the actual canvas. This art "is not *static*," he writes. "The *trace* makes it fluid... The more famous a work is, the more inscriptions it has." Han also observes that in China, two forms of "copy" exist: *fangzhipin*, meaning "imitations where the difference from the original is obvious" (such as a poster of a Rembrandt), and *fuzhipin*, "exact reproductions of the original, which, for the Chinese, are of equal value to the original." Fuzhipin have caused controversy outside China, such as in 2007 when Hamburg's Museum of Ethnology closed a touring exhibition of Chinese terra-cotta warriors when it discovered that the statues had been manufactured recently.

Such dissatisfaction is at once warranted and naive. In *Ways of Seeing*, art critic John Berger describes how copies of artworks appearing on television provide new, unique experiences to spectators that remove the "bogus religiosity" attached to works of art as cult objects.

Engaging with three-dimensional replicas is no different. Though they should always be identified as such, if constructed well, reproductions still elicit an emotional response and help provide insight into the past.

But the hierarchy between original and copy, if not nearly destroyed by the advent of photography and film, may be even more obsolete in the digital age: We now praise robots for their ability to "pass" as human, while online, the origin of data matters little outside security departments.

These contemporary truths aside, copies of works of art possess qualities that separate them from the originals: They are emotionless, made without risk, surprise or spontaneity. They are also only of the present.

In Berger's words, the gestures of the artist inscribed in the original, particularly in drawings and paintings, "close[s] the distance in time between the painting of the picture and one's own act of looking at it."

Beyond bridging historical divides, the original also brings the spectator into intimate contact with its creator. As writer Siri Hustvedt notes, when looking at art, "I am aware of another mind and body, a 'you' in relation to my 'I.'" Engaging with such works, she asserts, is an intersubjective experience—the kind of communal experience that every move toward the digital, the new and the endlessly reproducible, makes a little less possible.

Artwork: Float 01 by Paul Kremer

Moley Talhaoui

Meet the Swedish-Moroccan artist who set his dual identities on a creative collision course.

Photography: Lasse Fløde

Artist Moley Talhaoui didn't speak until he was four years old—a fact that worried his mother and the psychologists that she took him to, until they realized he was already including complex dimensions in his drawings: Talhaoui wasn't struggling to communicate, he was just more interested in doing so with pictures than with words. "I've always been like that," he says, shrugging.

From introverted child to self-taught painter, Talhaoui continues to channel his inner emotional state into a creative outpouring. Born in Sweden to Moroccan parents, his connection to two dramatically different cultures plays out in work that is arresting in its use of graphic imagery yet always restrained. Large canvases are covered with jarring depictions of skeletons and distorted human forms; swathes of color are contained by expanses of heavy black. "There's the totally free side from Morocco and the opposite from Sweden," he explains. "It's like organized chaos."

What was the first work of art that moved you? *Guernica* by Pablo Picasso. Something about that painting reminded me of myself and a poster of it stayed in my room until I left home at 18. For me, the dynamics in my paintings are almost always based on a feeling from *Guernica*. The theatrical vibe, the energy—if I can sense

that in something that I paint, I feel satisfied.

How do your Moroccan heritage and Swedish upbringing play out in your art? I'm not trying to build something based on visuals from history, but when I draw I think there's emoting within me that is connected to my ancestors. The Berbers are creative people, especially when it comes to music and art, while my Swedish identity is more about the ability to use less. It's a collision between being completely free and also being limited. The Moroccan side is that free spirit and the Swedish side is questioning and always going back and thinking it isn't good enough.

Your work often trades in mystical imagery. Are you religious? When I was growing up, my mom told me all these theological stories from Christianity and Judaism. But she never told me about any women who had the same status as the male prophets. As the child of a single mom that I looked up to like a goddess, it made me question religion—and that was the first step towards my personal enlightenment.

The concept of religion seems based on a book of answers to existential anxiety. All those questions are based on three thoughts: "What?" "Why?" and "Where am I?" If you can't answer those questions, anxiety can grow and grow

and you can feel quite lost, so I can see the natural instinct towards religion. I have a lot of anxiety—it's been there since I was a child and it's almost always based on those three questions. So when I paint, it's a relief for me. I can be in a state where I can relax and capture something from within.

Does that mean it's difficult to create work if you're happy? I would say I'm always in a state of conflict. If you think about it, everyone is: "Should I go out or should I stay in tonight? Should I have coffee or tea?"

When have you felt happiest? To feel happy, you need to have felt sorrow. It's kind of easy to feel euphoric but I think there's a misunderstanding of the concept of happiness. Happiness is when you don't have the need to feel anything. You're in the middle: You don't have desires, everything is okay. The only time I've really felt that—not by pursuing it or by trying to come to a balanced state of mind—is when I saw my son for the first time. That first second when I saw part of his skin felt like my mind was empty of the past and any wishes for the future. It was five seconds but it felt much longer. I wouldn't call it happiness, but nothingness—total stability.

What does it feel like when you paint? Have you heard about the

"It's self-centered or narcissistic to believe that one's own reality is an orchestra played by you."

Talhaoui says that if he wasn't an artist he would be a psychologist or a philosopher or he'd move to the Brazilian rainforest.

idea of "flow"? When you see the whirling dervishes doing it, it's referred to as a trance. It almost feels like everything that is happening around you in life is your own doing, but in the same moment you shut off and maybe feel a bit stupid or embarrassed for even thinking such a thing. It's kind of self-centered or narcissistic to stretch so far as to believe that one's own reality is just an orchestra played by you.

When I'm in my process and get to that state of mind, it becomes similar to that experience that I mentioned earlier about when I first saw my son—just a sense of *now*. There's that total freedom versus my humanity and vanity, which creates this conflicted energy in my work.

What's the best and the worst feedback that you've ever received? I met this guy through a friend. He looked at my work and said, "Oh, but you're lazy." That was maybe the best and the worst feedback. It was like I was nonchalant—that I could do whatever and that "it" thing in me would show. He saw that I didn't have respect for my work or those who would receive

it. Before that, if someone was to say something about me, whether it was good or bad, I didn't listen. But with him, I really felt a deep honesty with no agenda. I think that changed the course of my artistry. It made me realize that I had to be in shape.

Tell me about your tattoos. Do you design them? I have ideas and references but I don't design them. It feels like if I were to design my own tattoos it would be weird to appreciate them. Everything represents something but it's mostly based on the form or a decoration.

Would you advise your son to be an artist? Whatever he is, or becomes, that's his path. I don't want to project any ideas of what would please me onto him. He is perfect in that he just is. When you produce an identity that you need to live up to, that's where the big conflict starts within you. On some occasions, I feel like I need to respond to something based on my gender, my nationality, my culture or heritage. Whenever you have to think beforehand about how to respond, it's not natural. So whatever he is, it just adds to his completeness.

"To feel happy, you need to have felt sorrow."

Before the birth of his son, Talhaoui would often start new paintings in the middle of the night. Now that his routine is more circumscribed, he keeps a sketch pad with him to jot down ideas instead.

2
Features

Anh

A portrait of the painter in her West Village studio. Words by Laura Rysman & Photography by Billy Kidd

Duong

With rouged lips, red-lacquered nails, wide eyes and bowed brows that look inked by a fine-tipped brush, the artist Anh Duong sits on a velvet couch in her West Village apartment. Graceful and pole-straight like the ballerina she once was, Duong, now 57, is a rebuke to the notion that beauty belongs to the young. Behind her hangs a self-portrait—an almost gnarled reflection of herself in thigh-high stockings and garish smudges of makeup, a cluster of wilting, vulvic calla lilies gripped between her legs. One eye stares you down while the other, unnervingly, wanders. The 2008 painting *Philosophy and Prostitution* is Duong, but inside out.

Duong is a portraitist and, as her own most frequent subject, a diarist on canvas. She's painted famous friends, among them: Anjelica Huston, Susan Sarandon, Natalia Vodianova, Simon de Pury and Diane von Furstenberg (a work which was purchased by the National Portrait Gallery in Washington). She paints lesser-known characters as well, along with occasional still lifes of flowers, shoes, even breakfast. Self or other, something writhes in the paintings, an angst impossible to discern in her composed countenance.

"Art has always been about the male gaze," says Duong, as she leans back on the couch. "What's so great about being an artist now is that it's finally about the woman's gaze. It's finally about how we view beauty, desire, thoughts and ourselves." Duong, with her intimately personal portraits, seems more relevant than ever, but when she began her career in the late 1980s the skepticism was greater. Duong was not just an attractive young woman, but a famous model and the girlfriend of a very famous artist. She was, at first glance, easy to dismiss as a hobbyist.

The French-born daughter of a Spanish mother and Vietnamese father, Duong grew up outside of Paris, training throughout her youth to become a ballerina. At 22, she met the renowned fashion photographer David Seidner one night while partying at Paris' Palace club. He cast her in an Yves Saint Laurent campaign, her first modeling gig, and one of the most prestigious bookings possible. "I didn't fit into the beauty standard of that era when Christie Brinkley was the ideal," Duong observes. "But David put his stamp on my kind of beauty and made it fashionable." She was catapulted to muse status for many of the breakthrough designer talents of the 1980s—Dolce & Gabbana, John Galliano and Christian Lacroix—and became a regular on their runways.

"Artists create their own world. I was attracted to that freedom."

Styling: Debbie Hsieh, Hair/Makeup: Ashleigh Ciucci

"We all have doubts. We have to pretend we're so perfect and so fabulous, but who actually feels that way about themselves? No one."

In photos from the time, Duong is as elegant and attenuated as a designer's illustration, seeming to embody the most stylized opulence of the era's high fashion. However, she recalls it as a pose struck under rigid scrutiny. "As a model, the whole world is staring at you and saying what's right and what's wrong," she says with a grimace. Dance had already instilled in her a foundation of tense self-consciousness. "As a ballerina, you grow up judging yourself in front of a mirror, watching every millimeter." By 26, she considered herself to be aging out of modeling and decamped to New York City.

"Coming from ballet and modeling, I was craving having my own voice and my own vision," she explains—her voice betraying only the slightest French inflection, after now having spent more years in New York than in her native land. In the downtown New York of 1987, she found the art scene to be a flourishing wonderland of inventive, bohemian autonomy. "Artists create their own world. I was attracted to that freedom," she explains. Her mother had been a painter but abandoned the craft early on; Duong herself grew up painting, turning to self-portraiture even at a young age, though she never considered it a career possibility or contemplated art school. "As a kid, I was shy," she says. "I was in my dreams and in my head all the time. [Painting] was just a great way to process my inner world for someone who didn't know how to express things."

In New York, Duong found an urban cadre of free-spirited creatives. She met artists who were radically reshaping the art scene, including Francesco Clemente, George Condo, David Salle, Eric Fischl and Alex Katz (who would both paint Duong), and Julian Schnabel. Duong became the muse and girlfriend of Schnabel, an artist who had made a name for himself by painting portraits over smashed-up plates in a neo-expressionist style, and by introducing himself to people as "the most famous painter in America."

"He never taught me how to paint, but he saw the painter in me," says Duong. "He encouraged me to have a career as a painter, to live the artist's life, and when someone who's very successful gives you reassurance, it helps." During their five-year relationship, Duong and Schnabel lived together in a former chemical plant in the West Village where she painted until she later found her own studio. It was there that, side by side, they painted a friend, David Yarthu, who posed standing on a chair dressed for Halloween as a king in an ermine cape and crown. Duong used one of Schnabel's eight-foot canvases for her version of the portrait—a sad-eyed and childlike depiction of the man in his ersatz finery. Dennis Hopper stopped by the studio to visit Schnabel and fell for Duong's painting—it became her first sale. She continued to favor large-scale canvases from then on, and by 1990 she had her first solo show of 12 giant portraits at Sperone Westwater Gallery.

Duong was known as a model, as a beauty, as the girlfriend of an egotistical and larger-than-life artist. She found it easy to get attention, especially from *Vogue* and the fashion world, but obtaining critical acclaim was another matter. "The 1980s were so macho—everyone wanted to be Jackson Pollock," she says, standing up to stretch her legs across the living room. "Back then, most female artists had to look and act like guys to be taken seriously. I felt like I had to downplay modeling, being feminine, how I looked, even my personality, and I didn't want to pretend to be a man. I wanted to be authentic."

In an era when men were expected to relay the big ideas and universal truths of art, it's easy to understand why the idea of a star female model mostly painting herself was taken by some to be facile narcissism. However, Duong's portraits are the inverse of the serene loveliness that she exudes in her fashion photographs. Her body is often bared and painted without pleasing eroticism or romance. She peers out at viewers with a mix of unguarded emotions, reflecting the state of the self alone and uncircumspect—full of doubt, anguish, resentment, defiance, despair or even tedium.

Queenie Wong, a curator at New York's Sonnabend Gallery, which represents Duong today, reckons that "the most compelling and intriguing components of her self-portraits are the eyes. She gazes directly at the viewer, as if her true self is yearning for a connection, hoping to find a common ground through empathy." In a sexually charged painting from 2004, Duong squats on a fluffy fur rug wearing a lacy dress and heels, a dildo in her hand at the center of the canvas. The arrangement suggests an exchange of sensuality, but the title, *Il a repassé ma jupe (He ironed my skirt)*, suggests otherwise, and the expression on her face broadcasts a private, timid look of dispossessed hope.

Duong's paintings are her daily journals—notes taken on her state of being in the form of a portrait, neither flattering nor grotesque. "People ask me, why did you paint yourself so ugly?" she says, wrinkling her nose in displeasure. "But it's not about that. I was just expressing a lot of uncomfortable emotions. They can be quite hard to look back on for me," she sighs. "They're a testament to what I was feeling, and it leaves

As an actress, Duong appeared most recently in *Appropriate Behavior*, a rom-com in which she plays an Iranian expatriate whose daughter comes out as bisexual.

KINFOLK   49

Duong also had roles in movies including *Scent of a Woman, My Best Friend's Wedding* and *High Art.*

"In painting, I'm never vain or self-conscious. I don't care how I'm going to look."

me very exposed." Her practice is to put brush to canvas straightaway without first sketching what she'll paint, sitting herself in front of a true mirror (a mirror angled to reflect the actual image, rather than the image in reverse) and arranging herself with the garments and objects she feels attracted to on that day. "It's about trusting the dialogue with the subconscious," she says. "That's what's interesting about any creative process—your work will uncover something about you that you're not aware of consciously."

In the personal, Doung finds the universal. Her self-portraits are "not about painting myself," she says, but about revealing an intuitively recognized experience that will resonate with viewers in different ways. "The role of the artist is to create emotions in other people," she says. Though she began her painting career three decades ago, her unchanging message is more timely than ever, as a repositioning wave of feminism opens up space for women to narrate themselves, to be the directors and authors of the stories being told about themselves and to find, in those particularities, a new universality. It's a moment when there is more room not only for women, but for the candidly feminine.

"Painting has always been the place where I experience the most freedom," says Duong, leaning forward. "In painting, I'm never vain or self-conscious. I don't care how I'm going to look." After the physical perfection demanded by ballet and fashion, painting gave her footing in a world where she was in charge, where she directed herself, where the perhaps unsightly prospect of her inner reality could supersede the surface representation of herself. "Every self-portrait reflected another day, another emotion, another thing happening in my life," she says. "It was where I could finally express anxiety or fear, and remove this pressure I'd always had as a dancer and a model." Duong tried acting as well, gaining smaller parts in several movies, but says, "I always knew I needed to paint. The revelation came when I realized a person could live as an artist."

To paint is to meditate, she contends, and it comes with all the same difficulties and discipline: "There's no such thing as waiting for inspiration." You have to force yourself to start, you have to hurdle the noise in your head—your ego and your fears and your doubts, she says. "You have to push yourself out of the way to be true to yourself and to be true to the creative process." Although Duong owns an old fisherman's house out in East Hampton where she built herself a painting studio, she finds it "too beautiful and relaxing to paint there." She prefers to paint in her

West Village apartment—a handful of diminutive rooms once home to Mark Twain—where she has "the psychological drama that the city induces" and all of her props and clothes that she may need on hand.

The clothing in her paintings evokes femininity, modeling and fashion. But it also recalls the sartorial cues of more classical portraiture—and of the artists that have inspired Duong, like Goya, Velázquez and Manet—where brocades and laces serve to frame potent and unnerving characters. Even her nudes owe something to the audacity of Manet and his picnicking woman scandalously disrobed on the grass—a nude freed from the traditional, moralizing confines of mythological and biblical narrative depictions. But Duong's nudes tell her own story, a woman's story—a story with scant representation in the art world.

Thirty years into her career, she's still industriously pursuing her craft, painting and even sculpting self-portraits (a first for the artist) and she describes the last two years as some of the most work-intensive of her life. For the Statue of Liberty Museum that will open in 2019, Duong is sculpting a set of 50 gilded stars that will hang from the statue's restoration armature, gleaming in the entrance of the new institution.

In recent times, she's even returned to modeling for Pomellato, Bottega Veneta, Kate Spade and H&M, as transforming ideas about female representation brought in a wave of women well past the typical youthful ideal of the industry. "I felt so silly and superficial about modeling when I was young," Duong says. "It's just something you did because you're born a certain way, and you were just a face back then." Today, she points out, she's in demand as a model precisely because she's an artist, because she proves that "women over 40 have a life, that we deserve to have the right to age. Today I feel like a feminist when I'm modeling. We put shame on women for everything—like you're dirty because you're getting older." *Shame*, she repeats, her eyes narrowing. It's a powerful way to diminish women. "I'm happy we're seeing this start to change."

The pressure to please with the external and the desire to give voice to the internal is the tension that pushes and pulls women's lives. "I'm aware of my privileges," she says, "But we all have doubts. We have to pretend we're so perfect and so fabulous, but who actually feels that way about themselves? No one." Her expression has changed, her poised public face replaced with the vulnerable layers of private disquiet glimpsed in her paintings. "As an artist, what I'm interested in portraying is not me as a model, not the image of me that's been projected into the world, but the inside suffering, the contradiction."

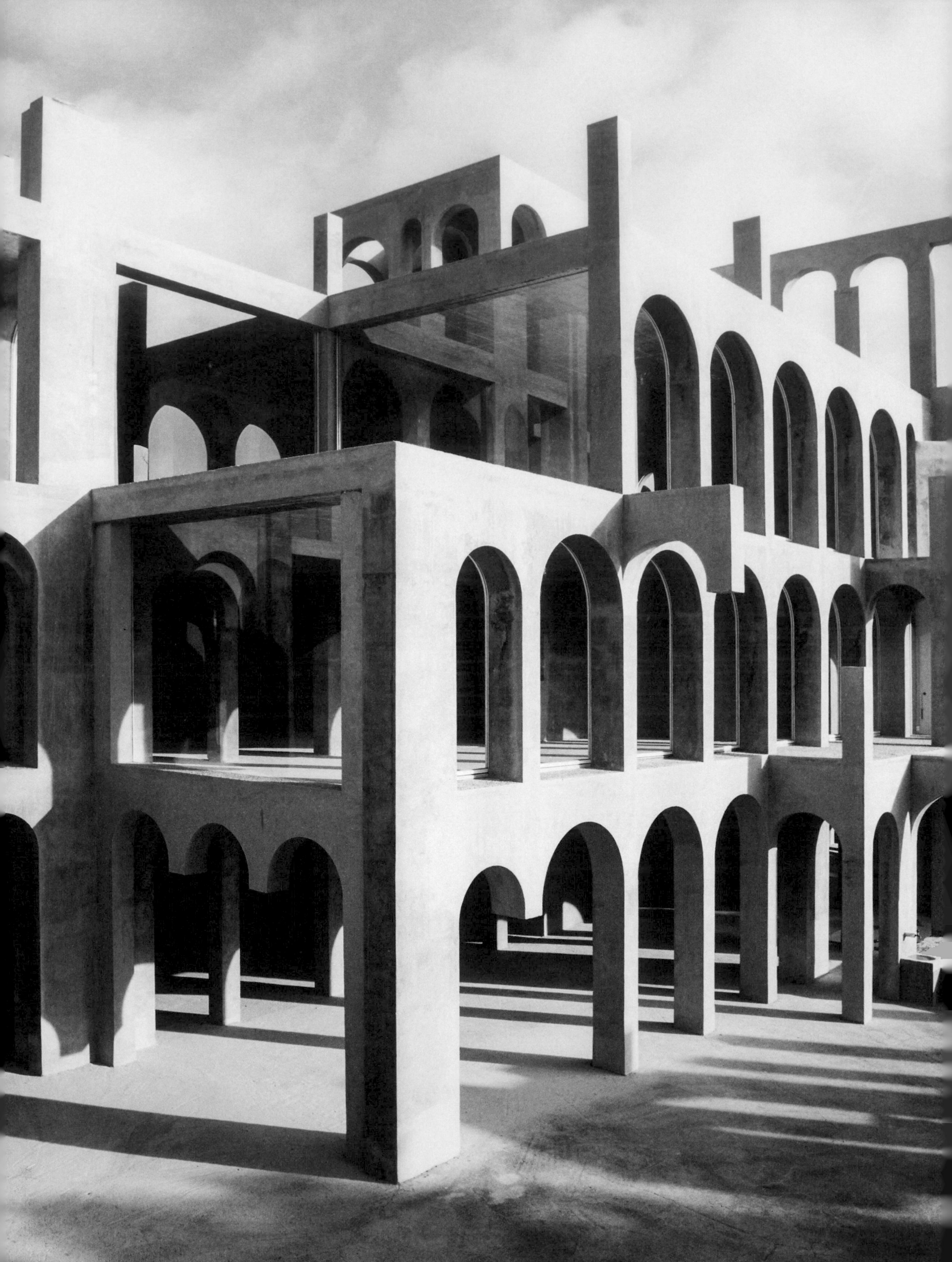

Xavier Corberó:
At the edge of Barcelona, an anomaly: a sculptor's labyrinthine home. Photography by *Salva López*

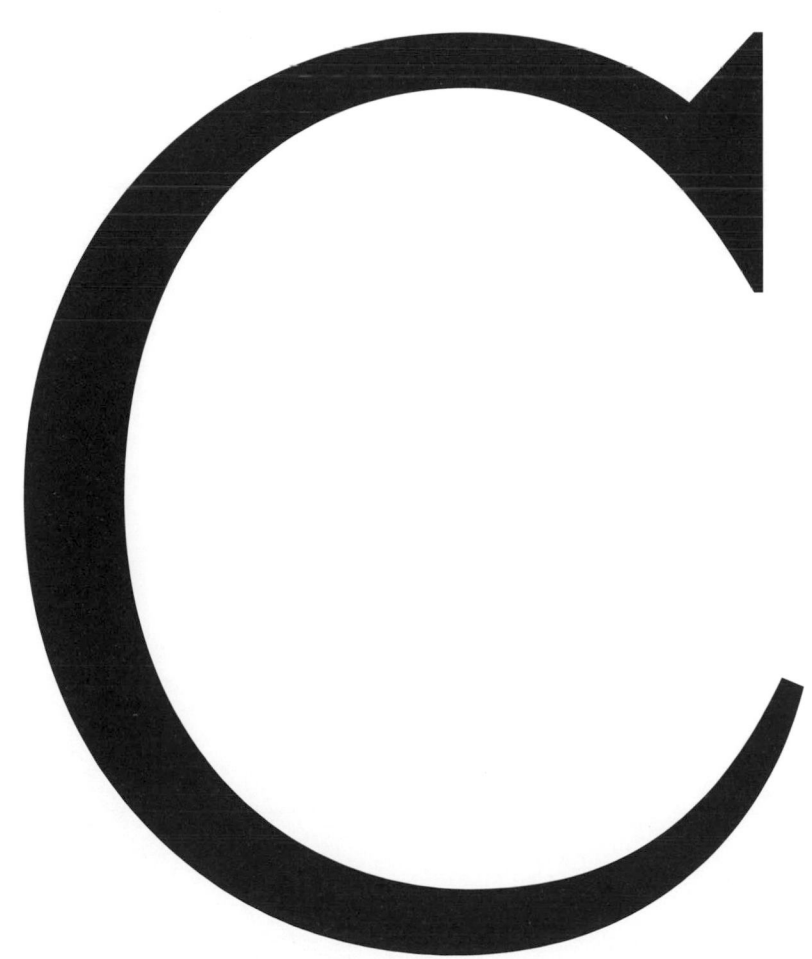

There is no logical pathway through *Xavier Corberó's* Barcelona estate, and no limits to its eccentricity other than those imposed by the laws of physics. Following Corberó's death last year, writer *Tristan Rutherford* explores the surreal masterpiece, and home, of one of Catalonia's most celebrated sculptors.

Corberó's monumental works—usually scuplted from basalt or marble—can be seen on the streets of London, Beirut, New York City and his beloved Barcelona.

On a former potato farm, Corberó planted floating staircases and hundreds of arches. "The outcome of what I do has to be poetry," he once said.

Xavier Corberó built what feels like the world's biggest kaleidoscope. At the epicenter of the sculptor's Catalan estate, a six-story structure rises like a contemporary Tower of Pisa. The interior of the tower is a hollow atrium; here, plants dangle and light spangles through arched windows, shining a surreal light show into a cathedral of modernism.

Corberó, who was born in 1935 and died last year, is one of Spain's most celebrated sculptors. However, his legacy does not primarily consist of his artworks—large standing structures, often hewn from rough rock—but rather his home: a madcap network containing dozens of dwellings, sprawling their way across an 11-square-mile site on the outskirts of Barcelona. When he died at the age of 80, he was still not finished with the creation of this private Neverland.

The six floors of the central tower once comprised Corberó's personal dwelling. These open-fronted rooms reveal an eclectic approach to decorating: A photograph of his friend, the surrealist artist Salvador Dalí, hides behind an ancient Chinese screen; a Le Corbusier chaise longue sits on an Arabian carpet. Other creations were hewn by Corberó's own hand

from polished basalt or pink marble. As the sunlight shifts around the central funnel of light, alternate items are highlighted piece by piece—as if paging through an art sales catalog.

Stretching out from the personal quarters are a network of rooms for entertaining and exhibiting—there are so many that Corberó would occasionally forget he had built certain annexes. He would hoodwink visitors with labyrinthine illusions like false walls and staircases that led into thin air. This was a project of two halves: one of the world's greatest private art museums, and an incomparable party pad.

It's hard to imagine Corberó's home existing anywhere other than Barcelona. When he was born, Spain was on the cusp of civil war. The ensuing censorship ran to books, journals and films. Tower blocks concreted over the old with visions of the new. Culture came from Madrid, not from the backwater of Barcelona. In short, if you wanted to see homegrown art, you had to create your own. And Corberó had a famous local role model to inspire him in this pursuit: Antoni Gaudí, who had created some of Barcelona's most famous architectural

monuments and had been a friend of his grandfather's. The Catalan modernist, who died in 1926, had set an inspiring precedent for the younger man—not just by dint of his ambitious, overreaching surrealism, but also by championing a form of design that promoted the region's anti-establishment identity through culture, architecture and art.

Corberó's first move was to purchase a crumbling *masia* that was scheduled to be demolished in order to make way for a highway intersection. In the late 1960s, *arte povera*—the anti-elitist movement that championed the use of everyday materials—was a necessity in dusty Catalonia. The masia's crude kitchen was painted using color samples. Catalan quarries that produced quartzy limestone and silicon-rich marble were scoured for art supplies. Contemporary art was created with timeless materials, sourced from the earth yet strikingly modern. Standing stones were piled in threes to look like lines of commuters—a design that Corberó continued to favor even at the height of his fame as a sculptor.

Corberó's madcap maze was built up around this simple dwelling. An estate of interconnected

The estate sprawls over 48,000 square feet and evolved over a period of 40 years. It is a home, Corberó said, "in which the mental space—not the real one—is what matters."

homes rose in Moorish modern style. Some were silhouetted husks of Arabesque curves. Others featured monastic, whitewashed walls that cloistered a growing collection of contemporary furniture. As ever, old met new. Hardwood doors echoed Spain in the 17th century, yet some magically swung open by remote control.

The more Corberó's work became acclaimed, the harder he laughed. Salvador Dalí telephoned to purchase a piece, but the sculptor thought it was a crank call and told the surrealist that he was a bishop, before hanging up the phone. A brick wall was built around a vintage Rolls-Royce, which gave visitors sleepless nights as they wondered how on earth the vehicle got inside. The kaleidoscopic tower rose above the estate, with Corberó's poetic light beams burnishing his ever-growing anthology of art. The rambling mansion had places to party, parley and pontificate. Scores of local guests—poets, dancers, painters, dilettantes—turned the *casa* into a Catalonian salon. Private dinners with Norman Foster could take place in any number of nooks, as the property took on the expansive dimensions of a Bond villain's lair. Another corner of Corberó's hollow tower home became the ideal place in which to place an armchair: "I wanted there to be a spot from which almost everything can be seen," he said. His house, his rules. Photos of Corberó taken in situ show a pensive artist wearing a corduroy jacket with suede shoes, offset by a pair of shocking pink socks. In art, in architecture, in style, there was always juxtaposition.

Daniel Riera, a photographer and filmmaker who uses Corberó's work as a set, witnessed the same zany pageant. "The house is like a dreamed up landscape from a futurist art painting," he says. For Riera, the magic doesn't lie in the luxury of the elements, but in the way interiors and exhibits meld with each other. Marble balls and black metal spires rest on untreated wood floors (other similar pieces from Corberó's opus are in London's Victoria & Albert Museum and New York's Metropolitan Museum of Art). "Inside it's a kind of imagined space of extreme photogenia," says Riera. "But the trick is that you can't guess from outside what wonders you can find within." Indeed, the property's skyline—viewed from the outside—is no different from other buildings in the Barcelona suburb of Esplugues de Llobregat.

Corberó was present, though nonintrusive, during some of Riera's shoots for the likes of Spanish retailer Mango and interiors magazine *Apartamento*. This dovetails with the laissez-faire oversight he gave those who visited on his art residency programs. Painters and sculptors were welcome to work in cloistered solitude for anything from six months to six years. "They are here to find themselves, not me," he once remarked.

Yet he used his influence to spotlight dozens of young artists. As Barcelona wowed the world during the 1992 Olympics, Corberó was commissioned to install local street art across a city reborn. For the opening ceremony, where the Olympic hymn was sung in Catalan, Corberó was also asked to design the winners' medals. The motif he used was three scrawled lines representing a jumper leaping the Olympic rings. It's runic and elemental. And it captures the artist's power to bewitch with simple strokes on materials cast from the earth.

A spell was also cast over Sandy Brunner, a Barcelona-based Swiss architect, who leads private tours of the estate. "When we visit we might meet Corberó's manager or widow," she says. "These people bring the place alive with stories." One artwork they point guests toward is *The Smoker*, a sculpture conveniently leaning by the doorway so he can puff outside. The property's labyrinthine structure makes every one of Brunner's tours a fresh journey into an Escher-like whirlwind of art. "The result is a magic of illusion, although you are never really lost," she says. (The guest who recalls being obliged to call Corberó on his cell phone some years ago in order to locate him within the estate might disagree.)

Corberó's legacy is even harder to pinpoint. As Brunner neatly notes, "his art was like architecture, and vice versa." It's a style that could have continued in new directions had he opened other projects in the pipeline, which included a restaurant and hotel. His pen and sketchpad remain in the house as he left them, creating to the last. "The statues inside are now the inhabitants of the Corberó house," concludes Brunner. Perhaps his finest work was the property he built to house them in—an unfinished symphony to surrealism.

"The house is like a dreamed up landscape from a futurist art painting."

The home has 25 bedrooms; before his death, Corberó had wanted to establish a hotel.

CORBERÓ IN THE CITY

by Harriet Fitch Little

Corberó's sculptures, like his home, are extravagant in their scale and vision but unfussy in their execution; his basalt rock figures evoke the shape of the human form with a few blunt strokes of the chisel. Perhaps it is because of this rough-and-ready charm that Corberó's sculptures have proved particularly popular among city planners looking to inject slick and sanitized urban environments with something rawer. In downtown Dubai, 10 of Corberó's larger-than-life figures are clustered together in a gleaming public square, the Burj Khalifa towering directly behind them. Surprisingly, given his personal preference for designs that seem to be hewn from the ground on which they are built, he loved the location of the Dubai installation when it was unveiled in 2011, describing the Burj Khalifa as "the most beautiful building in the world."

THE EVOLUTION OF SELF-CARE

TEXT:
PAMELA K. JOHNSON

Self-care is big business. Go online, and you'll find a $40 vegan candle, a $70 aromatic diffuser and a $110 face oil being marketed as "me time" essentials. Yet the origins of the movement are to be found far away from hubs of commerce— among civil rights activists for whom the body was a site of political conflict. How did the conversation about self-care shift from society's radical margins—and the community activism of the Black Panther movement—into the indulgences of an individualized mainstream? Pamela K. Johnson charts the transition.

Before her 50th birthday, Audre Lorde faced cancer for the second time. The black feminist poet had already lost a breast to the disease, and six years later it doubled back for her liver. Though stunned by pain and fear, she declined medical intervention, and instead embraced her own form of self-care: keeping an appointment to teach in Germany, taking in the first Feminist Book Fair in London, and having fun. "I may be too thin," she noted in her journal, "but I can still dance."

Lorde died in 1992, but not before putting self-care on the map with her book of essays, *A Burst of Light*. In it she wrote: "Caring for myself is not self-indulgence, it is self-preservation, and that is an act of political warfare." In one of her journals, she took the idea further: "I wasn't supposed to exist anyway, not in any meaningful way in this fucked-up whiteboys' world." Coming of age during the civil rights movement, she observed that those marginalized by dint of class, sex or race often had to do battle just to get their basic needs met.

Some think of self-care as an hour at the nail salon or a day at the spa. But over the centuries, those who have advanced our understanding of the concept often did so as they tilted toward the blades of what felt like an indifferent world. Facing imminent danger, they gained clarity not just about surviving, but thriving. The personal became political: They sought to show that there is a relationship between self-care and a life well lived.

In the 1960s, the Black Panther Party organized in Oakland, California, specifically to

check police abuses against poor black citizens. The group's membership consisted of recent migrants whose families had fled to Northern and Western cities to escape the Southern racial regime. But when they got there, they were "confronted with new forms of segregation and repression," according to Donna Murch in her book, *Living for the City*. As the Panthers patrolled neighborhoods, they witnessed other needs going unmet. They evolved from protecting black bodies to uplifting black lives, and established medical and legal clinics, ambulance services and a program to feed children.

The Panthers' Free Breakfast for School Children program started in 1969. Initially held at one local church, it went from feeding a few kids to a few hundred to thousands daily in at least 45 locations around the US. "The school principal came down and told us how different the children were," said a parishioner who helped out in the early days. "[The kids] weren't falling asleep in class, they weren't crying with stomach cramps."

The Panthers' good deeds did not go unpunished. An armed band of black men and women (even during an open-carry era) did not sit well with American authorities. The FBI labeled the Panthers a hate group, and went after the party's reputation in part by attacking their community work, claiming the meals they served were infected with disease. They harassed children and parents who participated in the programs, and even destroyed food the night before a program was to open in Chicago. By planting moles to infiltrate the organiza-

tion and by staging violent raids against it, the FBI ultimately brought about the party's demise. But the free breakfast program refused to die. It drew attention to the fact that many American children had been going to school hungry. In the early 1970s, the US Department of Agriculture launched its free breakfast program, which has fed tens of millions of children over the years.

After free breakfasts became social welfare policy, other facets of the civil rights movement's approach to self-care started to be absorbed into the mainstream.

At the Behavioral Wellness Clinic in Mansfield, Connecticut, founder Monnica Williams has witnessed the transformation of self-care from radical political movement to an institutionalized staple of mainstream medicine. Yet she and her staff of therapists still encounter resistance, even when they prescribe what would seem to be enjoyable "homework" to their depressed or anxious patients: "We encourage them to do something in line with their values and goals," she says. "[But] it's often easier to get OCD [obsessive compulsive disorder] patients to touch trash cans as a part of their homework assignment than it is to get depressed patients to incorporate things that nurture them in their daily lives."

Williams admits that she herself wrestles with getting the proper quotient of self-care. An academician who has the whole summer off, she never takes more than a couple of weeks of vacation. That's not unlike many Americans, who in 2016 left more than 650 million vacation days in the bank. Williams suspects that the mindset of self-denial is a hard one to shake. "It goes back to our Protestant work ethic, when we were on the frontier," she notes. "But we're not on the frontier anymore."

The psychologist's work dovetails with that of the pioneering researcher Dorothea Orem, an American nurse who, between 1959 and 2001, developed the widely used "self-care deficit nursing theory." She identified self-care as a human need, and mentored health providers in supporting patients' desire to be as independent as possible, which improved outcomes in both rehabilitation and primary-care settings.

While self-help literature used to be dominated by authors recommending various techniques for self-improvement, recent years have seen a rise in books asking simply that we learn to care for what we have. Gay Norton Edelman is the author of one of them, *The Hungry Ghost: How I Ditched 100 Pounds and Came Fully Alive*, and she's at work on a second, *The Well-Fed Ghost*.

The writer remembers a difficult period when, as a young mother, she and her husband welcomed their third son. Exhausted by trying to meet the emotional needs of three small children, the stress overtook her. She found herself yelling at the boys for the smallest infraction, and simultaneously eating her way to a 100-pound weight gain. "I turned to food as a form of love," she recalls. That became a form of self-abuse, and she reached 254 pounds.

"I went to a therapist about it, and she said that what I needed as an antidote to yelling at the children was self-care. I literally didn't know what she meant," Norton Edelman recalls. She sought help with a sensible eating plan, and lost the excess weight in 14 months' time. But keeping it off and achieving a deeper sense of peace required a more mindful form of intervention. She found that her therapist's prescription of self-care was the right solution, and took simple steps such as taking time to put on lotion after a bath, or embarking on tech-free nature jaunts with her husband in New York's Adirondack Mountains. She also became more careful about not giving too much of herself away: "I have a magnet on my fridge that says: 'Somebody please stop me before I volunteer again.'"

Author John Crawford says he once lost an entire decade to anxiety. Over time, he found the ability to say "no" an important tool in not allowing himself to become overburdened. "One aspect of my own self-care, which I do hold incredibly important, is a commitment to not overdoing it in terms of working on things that exhaust me," says the author of *Anxiety Relief: A Thorough Self-Care Manual for Anxiety, Stress, and Panic*. "I am very mindful of my energetic limitations and extremely strict with ensuring that I don't overstep them." He arrived at this understanding after a psychotic episode upended his sanity. The UK-based therapist fell in love with a woman from the US. But after they married, they encountered financial,

mental and emotional hurdles in securing her residency in England. Crawford buckled under the strain. "As I paddled my way back to land, I learned about the ocean and mapped the territory," he writes. Along the way, he transformed from anxiety sufferer, to anxiety expert, to author who writes often on the subject as a way to aid others and spare them the agony he endured.

Crawford's rocky journey impressed upon him the value of sitting with difficult emotions. "It's quite natural to want to run away from horrible feelings," he explains. "Unfortunately, the act of trying to run away from them creates more tension within the body, which is what creates anxiety and depression in the first place." By attending to one's emotional pain with a degree of empathy and compassion, he's found that feelings can soften and even dissolve over time.

The current elevation of taking care of one's self has many historical precedents. The Ancient Greeks embraced *philautia*, or "love of self." Aristotle suggested that "all friendly feelings for others are an extension of man's feelings for himself," while his countryman Socrates posited, "a man should not attempt political leadership until he had attended to himself."

What also becomes clear, whether we look back to history or around at our contemporaries, is that self-care has always been closely linked to the existence of power imbalances. Gandhi, who staged numerous hunger strikes to protest oppression under colonial rule, un-

> "Some think of self-care as an hour at the nail salon or a day at the spa. Those who have advanced our understanding often did so as they tilted toward the blades of what felt like an indifferent world. Facing imminent danger, they gained clarity not just about surviving, but thriving."

derstood that the body was a battleground. When setting out his 12-point plan for India's independence from Great Britain, he included discussion of health and hygiene alongside his more famous doctrine of nonviolence. He also advocated disciplined self-preservation. "A 'no' uttered from the deepest conviction," he said, "is better than a 'yes' uttered merely to please, or worse, to avoid trouble."

His understanding of the body as a site of political power anticipated the work of French philosopher Michel Foucault. Foucault explored the structures of discipline and control within society, and offered his own insights into *le souci de soi* (concern for one's self). Foucault said that successfully fulfilling one's own needs requires reflection, meditation and practices that lead toward an ideal state of being. "To care for one's self is to know one's self," he asserted.

Sisters Nadia Narain and Katia Narain Phillips published *Self-Care for the Real World* in late 2017 because, Nadia says, "it was needed, especially at this time politically and socially." (In fact, the day after Donald Trump became president, Google searches on the subject of self-care shot up by 500 percent.) Nadia explains, "It starts with taking care of ourselves, our families, our street, our communities and allowing that to spread wider."

She is one of London's leading yoga teachers, while Katia is a body worker who started London's first raw food café in 2000. The two have been incorporating self-care into their teachings and retreats for a while. Over the years, though, they saw that while people were doing a lot of the right things for their health, they seemed to do so out of a sense of obligation. "It was restrictive and rigid. We were like that too... trying to purge ourselves in some way. It took us some time to recognize that we were being really tough on ourselves, but really nice to other people," says Nadia.

Some people view self-care, itself, as narcissistic. In a 2016 *Commentary* article on the subject, Christine Rosen points to Instagram posts that feature "people relaxing in bubble baths and performing other rigorous acts of wellness" as reductive, commercially driven understandings of the movement. For advocates of self-care, she goes on, "recovery doesn't mean bouncing back from a serious drug addiction or major surgery. They're recovering from having to navigate the realities of adulthood—experiences that previous generations understood as part of life's sometimes unpleasant facts, like having to save money." She suggests that people who spend an inordinate amount of time reacting to stress by journaling their "feeling words" won't develop the mettle to handle "the challenges of what is likely to be a long battle against global terrorism or economic and political upheaval."

But millennials of all stripes have embraced self-care as a lifestyle more than any generation before them. The Pew Research Center reported in 2015 that they spend twice as much as baby boomers on workouts, diets, coaching, therapy and well-being apps. Brianna Wiest, who was born in the 1990s and is a sought-after speaker and author of the poetry book *Salt Water*, offers insights as to why:

"Millennials were raised with a sense of self-worth and value that other generations weren't. They were told that they could be anything," she says.

At the same time, Wiest urges that people not fool themselves by going for self-care lite—soft, pampering strokes that fail to get down into the deep tissues where the real work must be done. "If you find yourself having to regularly indulge in consumer self-care, it's because you're disconnected from *actual* self-care," Wiest says. She advises increasing one's capacity to delay gratification, stepping outside of the comfort zone, and taking on the less glossy tasks that are required to grow in meaningful ways.

A self-care regimen based on who we are and what we need can steady us for those times when the blades of life tilt toward us and draw blood: traumas such breakups, job losses or the death of a loved one. In the case of Audre Lorde, her self-prescribed self-care helped her live more fully even as death was imminent, allowing her to peer through a philosophical lens to observe that, though cancer would win this battle, it would not win the war.

"For the first time I really feel that my writing has a substance and stature that will survive me," she wrote in a journal. "We all have to die at least once. Making that death useful would be winning for me."

Day in the Life:
Shirin Neshat

There are many ways in which to be a political artist. For *Shirin Neshat,* poetry, calligraphy and cinematography can convey stories of female disempowerment more powerfully than "shock art." *Charles Shafaieh* pays a visit to the home of one of New York's most widely recognized artists. Photography by *Zoltan Tombor*

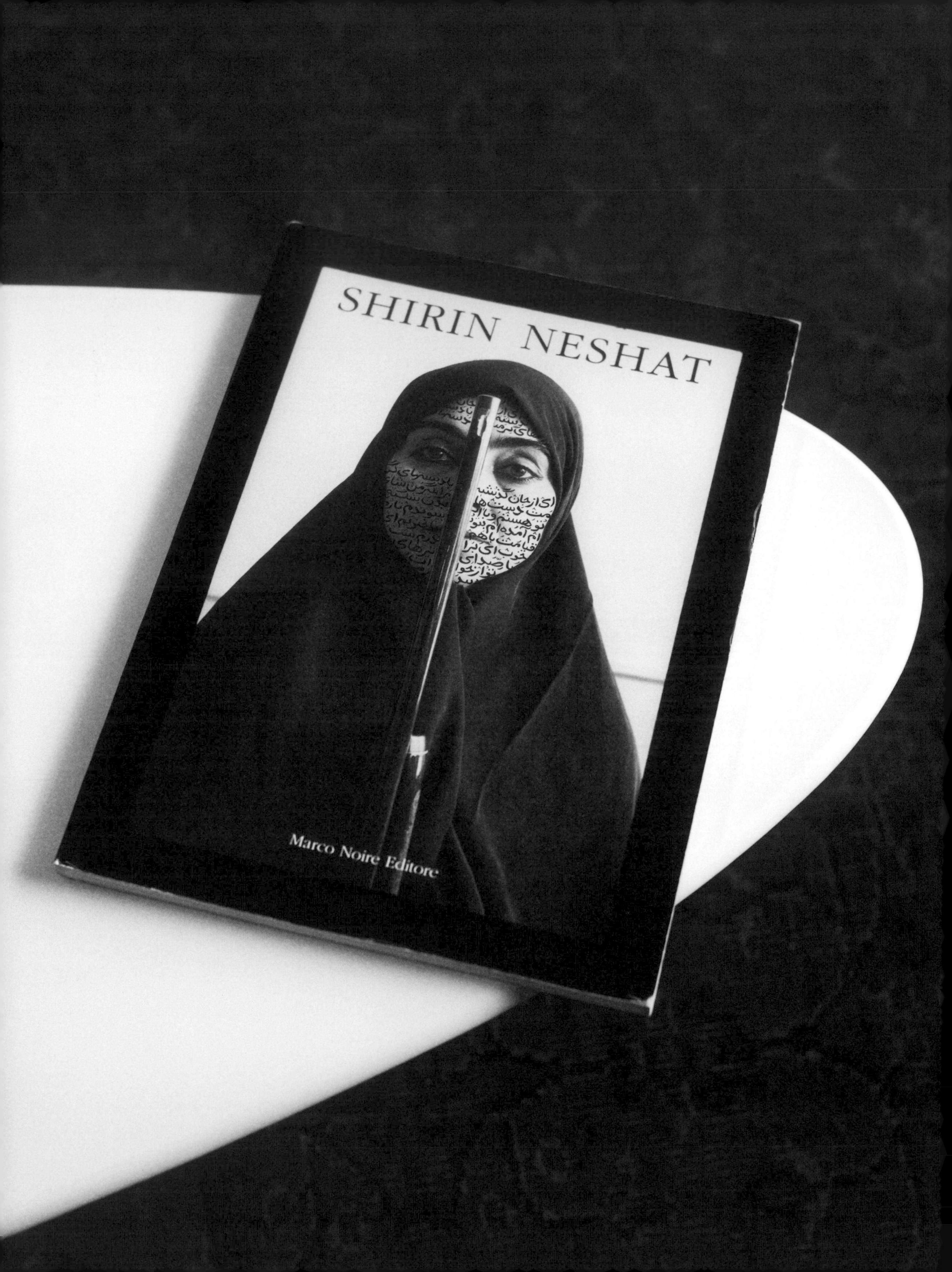
SHIRIN NESHAT
Marco Noire Editore

Art for art's sake is of no interest to Shirin Neshat. The Iranian-American artist mines the iconography, history and poetry of her homeland to explore both local and universal issues, from the chador and female body to ritual and performance. The video installations, calligraphy-lined photographs and live-performance work that results challenges the expectations and assumptions of Iranian and American, Muslim and atheist audiences alike. And she has made the leap from art to cinema: In 2010, her film about the 1953 coup in Tehran, *Women Without Men*, was an art house hit.

Neshat's work often takes her away from her apartment, as she meets the many collaborators with whom she has formed an international collective producing, assisting and even starring in each other's work. Despite this near-constant movement, Neshat remains attuned to quiet moments of beauty. When we spoke at her Brooklyn home and studio, she was transfixed by her Labrador, Ashi, who stared silently at a bird fluttering on the other side of a window. "That is something special," she says, her eyes brightening.

Do you have a daily routine? I'm very repetitious about everything I do. I wake up early, around 6:30 a.m., and have the most clarity in the morning. I eat breakfast, answer emails. I have a ritual of calling my mother in Tehran every day at 9 a.m. Then I try to prepare for work, because people arrive around 10:30 a.m. I make sure I'm quiet during this time, because when my team comes, it gets very busy. Then in the evening, I take dance classes—I'm obsessive about studying dance—and go out with friends or see movies. I don't ever work at night.

Managing both a public and private life can be difficult, especially in New York. It's really difficult to balance. I'm a workaholic; I work seven days a week. My personal life is mainly around my son, who lives in New York—I try to be really selfish about making time with him. There are times when I feel that the work takes over, but I try to rely on my home, my partner Shoja [Azari], my dog and my close friends.

My immediate group of friends are also collaborators. Since I started making films and met a community of Iranian friends and others—visual artists, theater directors, cinematographers, painters, writers, singers—it has become an experience to support each other. I feel not just a responsibility but a great satisfaction that the relationship between us is reciprocal. If I could use anything in my power to help them, why not?

It has always suited me very well to work with someone else—someone with whom to brainstorm and go through the journey together. I've never been one to just sit against a wall and paint.

That sense of artistic community is increasingly absent in Manhattan. When did you leave for Brooklyn? About a year ago. We lived in a very elegant SoHo loft but, after 18 years, we felt it was time to move on because the area has become so corporate. We wanted to incorporate our studio into our living area, too. Bushwick, our new neighborhood, is where artists are moving, and it's a very diverse area—very much like the East Village when I first moved to New York in 1983.

New York has become more clean-cut. The whole notion of bohemia doesn't really exist here anymore. The underground artists doing crazy projects and performance pieces are not in galleries in Chelsea, which are clean and cold. You feel it's all about the dealers and collectors, as opposed to the artists. In some ways, I come from the blue-chip gallery world—I'm represented by one of the best galleries, I'm friends with many important artists—but I'm not into showing up at every opening, trying to meet collectors or be at the right place at the right time.

There's still lots of activity happening though, especially in Brooklyn. There are pockets of bohemian life and groups of artists here who are not at the center, which is very promising.

Looking for Oum Kulthum is Neshat's latest feature film, produced with her closest collaborator—her partner Shoja Azari. Neshat inserted herself into the narrative: The plot follows an Iranian filmmaker as she embarks on a biopic of the Egyptian icon.

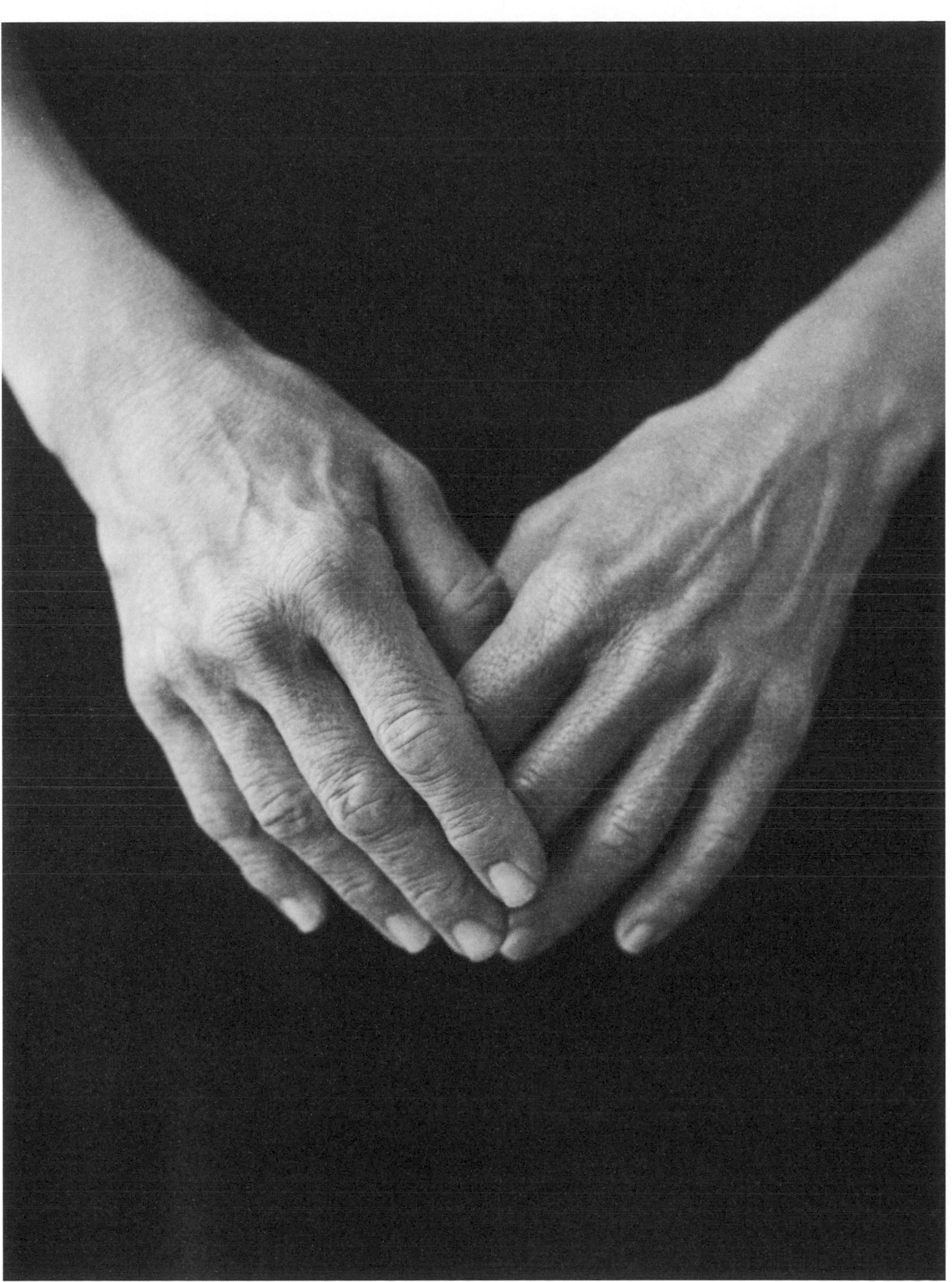

Too polished an environment doesn't allow for chaos and messiness to meld with beauty and order, which is something very important to your work. Is that true for your life as well? Living in places that are too comfortable is anticlimactic for artists. For example, I really don't enjoy going to fancy, trendy, very expensive restaurants—there's too much pretense. I like places that are rough, loud, crazy, chaotic, down-to-earth. It's similar to why I like Bushwick: There are rats here and garbage there, but you see beautiful scenes of mothers holding children's hands going to school in uniforms, or crazy-looking artists walking around at 3 a.m., and heroin addicts. You see life as it is.

As an artist, you need to be confronted by the good and the bad, the order and chaos. Too much chaos or too much order is problematic. I like something in-between. Trying to balance that, every day, keeps me on my edge and feeling like I'm still a young emerging artist as opposed to feeling safe. Every day is a bit of a struggle and a challenge—I'm addicted to it. The projects I choose are very ambitious and almost impossible at times, and they can be very painful. I think that I subconsciously put myself in places where I'm testing myself.

Limitations—like those enforced upon artists living under oppressive regimes—can also engender better art than comfortable environments. I'm a strong believer that limitations lead to a very creative process. When you're within these parameters, in which so many things are not possible, you become very creative and imaginative to find solutions. In my work, I always enforce a set of boundaries in terms of what I will and will not do, which helps me. If infinity were the limit, I would just be lost! I don't mean to overgeneralize, but I think that's forgotten by Western artists, because pretty much everything—from nudity to insulting political leaders and religion—is acceptable in art for them.

"I've never been one to just sit against a wall and paint."

Previous page: Shirin wears a sweater by COS. Left: She wears a shirt and skirt by Hermès. Right: She wears a turtleneck by Sandro and skirt-trousers by COS.

American photographer Cindy Sherman was the first person to buy Neshat's work in 1995. Neshat, who has long cited Sherman as a major influence, considers it the high point of her career.

"Everything you're not allowed to say overtly you can say through poetry."

Critics often ignore work if it isn't overtly political. Even artists become conscious about what succeeds. But I often think about artists like Paul Thomas Anderson, whose films are not politically relevant but are existentially important. It's a mixed blessing when you make art that has an acute relationship with political ideas. On the one hand, it's sexy, provocative, sensational; on the other, the theme takes over the form, and the subject dominates the art. My work tries to keep a balance between deeply poetic, universal and timeless issues.

Poetry and music are means by which you've shown how limitations can be transcended. Why do you keep returning to those two elements? Music is a kind of pure emotion. I've used it in most of my work because most of my subjects are very silent, coming from oppressive lives. To have a voice as a musician is very symbolic because music transcends reality and its issues. There is a way to be expressive with music that you cannot be in normal conversation.

Similarly, the poetry written on my images is meant to arouse emotions and be very subversive, in a way suggesting the voice. Most Iranian people use poetry as a form of reflection, with somewhat mystical inclinations, and also to be subversive—because everything you're not allowed to say overtly you can say through poetry. It's very allegorical and metaphoric. That's the main thing that I appreciate about poetry: It's not direct and also so significant in what it means.

Dreams appear frequently in your work, too. I'm fascinated by dreams and try to write mine down immediately. There are always references to reality—places you've been and people you know—but also things that bother you, anxieties, fears that you don't usually like to think about. I like that they're very abstract.

I've made many videos of my dreams and my next film—a kind of surrealistic, absurd political satire on the Iran/America tension but also a critique of poverty in America—will be called *Dreamland*. It's about an Iranian woman, living in a very poor rural town in the Midwest, who is a census worker. She goes door-to-door to collect information, and at the end of each interview, she asks, "What was your last dream?" She makes it sound like it's part of the usual questionnaire. But then she gets back on the highway and drives to a surrealistic Iranian colony where there's an institution for the interpretation of Americans' dreams. So she's a spy who brings dreams!

Do you carry memories of your childhood in Iran with you? I'm always more nostalgic about those moments when I was just meandering through my father's fruit farm and the garden, when the spring would come with the scent of the blossoms. I don't have nostalgia about school or friends but more so environments—my home, my hometown. These things I remember very vividly.

SEATED

Photography by *Jean-Marie Franceschi*, Styling by *Barbara Gullstein* & Casting by *Sarah Bunter*

Models—some with two legs, some with four—sit for their portraits.

Previous page: Eames LCW by Charles & Ray Eames (1946) from Paustian. Adrian wears a suit by Mads Nørgaard, shirt by Sand Copenhagen
and shoes by Red Wing. Left: Thula wears a blazer by Tôteme. Above: Thonet 209 Armchair by Gebrüder Thonet (1900).
Adrian wears a knit by Armor Lux, trousers by Vivienne Westwood and shoes by Red Wing.

Above: BM62 Armchair by Børge Mogensen (1957). Adrian wears a turtleneck by Sand Copenhagen. Right: Piano Chair by Vilhelm Wohlert (1955). Thula wears a blouse by COS and trousers by Malene Birger.

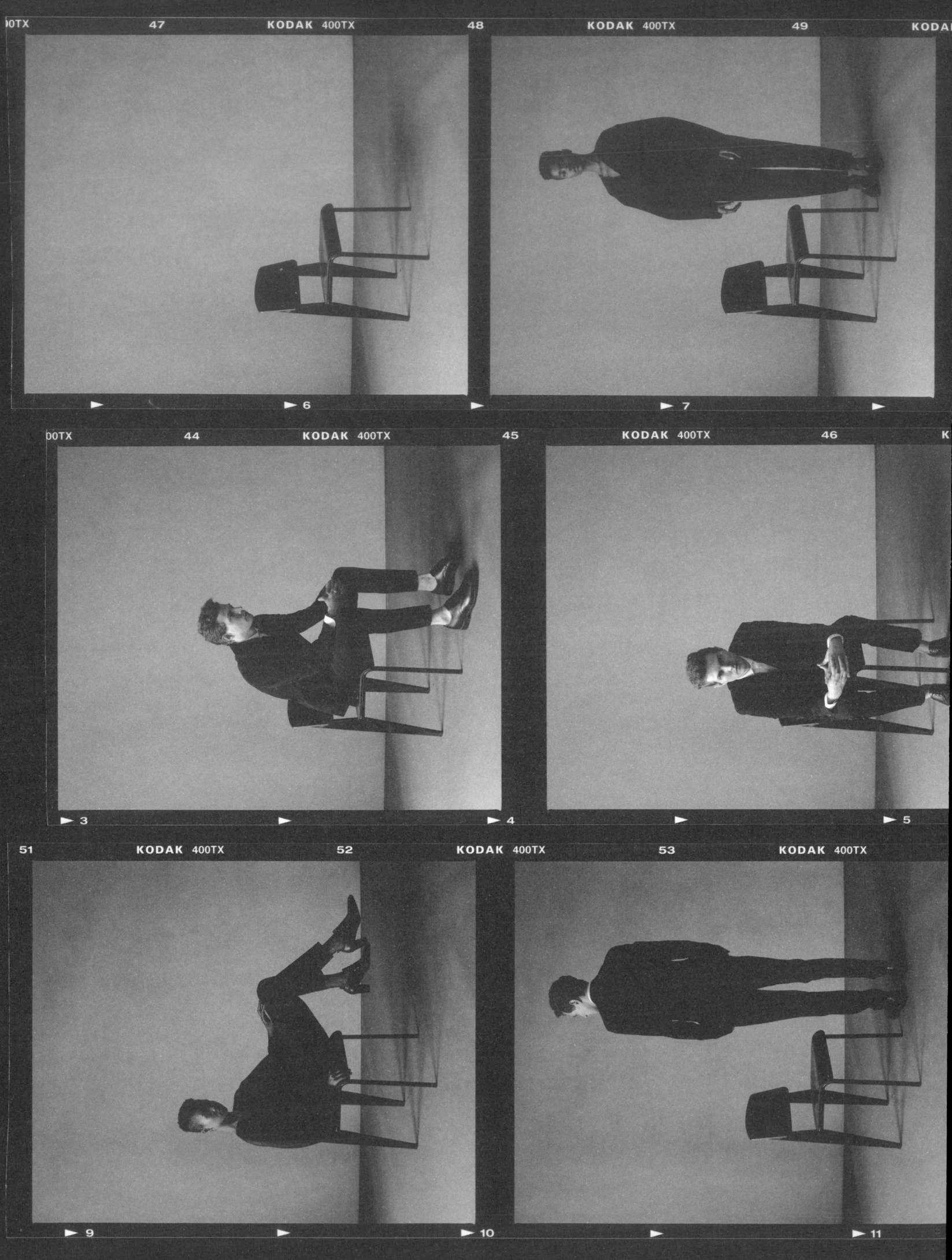

Standard Chair by Jean Prouvé (1934) from Paustian. Adrian wears a shirt by Sand Copenhagen, a blazer by Mads Nørgaard and shoes by Red Wing. Thula wears a blazer and trousers by Tôteme, shoes by Fiorella Pratto and a ring by Haniel.

Above: Standard Chair by Jean Prouvé (1934) from Paustian. Thula wears trousers by Tôteme and shoes by Céline. Right: LC1 Outdoor by
Le Corbusier, Pierre Jeanneret and Charlotte Perriand (1928) from Paustian. She wears a blazer by Tôteme.

Left: Thula wears a cardigan by Jacquemus and earrings by Haniel. Above: Piano Chair by Vilhelm Wohlert (1955). She wears blouse by COS and trousers by Malene Birger.

Mr.

Benjamin Booker grew up in a Tampa trailer park where his white neighbors once burned a cross on the family's lawn. *Kyla Marshell* meets the "kid from Florida" who decided to bear witness through music. Photography by *Emman Montalvan* & Styling by *Sue Choi*

Booker

Above: Booker wears a jumpsuit by Topman. Right: He wears a jacket by Topman, a T-shirt by Sunspel and trousers by COS.

If you saw an image of the musician Benjamin Booker out of context, you might think he was an actor from a civil rights–era period piece. With a vintage image to match his throwback sound—a rock-soul-blues amalgam that's earthy and analog—he has a style and countenance recalling Harry Belafonte, somewhere between worldly and weary.

Civil rights, and what we do with them, have been heavy on Booker's mind over the last few years. In 2017, he released his second full-length album, *Witness*, on ATO Records. The rousing title track, featuring Mavis Staples, evokes all the things that potent word might make you think of: gospel (as in, "Can I get a witness?"); bearing witness through truth-telling; and seeing that which you can't unsee.

For Booker, 29, a turning point in his relationship to many forms of witnessing was the death of Trayvon Martin in 2012, a few hours from where he lived in Gainesville, Florida. Though Booker knows exactly how many times he was stopped by police himself while in Gainesville (nine), he had believed he could escape the tragedy that had befallen other black people up until that moment. In a way, he saw himself as shielded. "I think I was just feeling kind of cocky," he says. "You're just like, 'I'm fine, I'm in college. They're not after me.' But nobody's safe."

Witness sprang not only from Booker's slow-moving epiphany about racism's personal effect on him, but also from the side effects of the success of his self-titled 2014 debut album. He went on tour with fellow blues-punker Jack White; appeared on the *Late Show with David Letterman*; and was named an "artist you need to know" by *Rolling Stone*. But the heady nature of his new life sent him into the arms of excess, where, among other things, he briefly found himself with a substance abuse problem. Seeking a break from the rock-and-roll pace his life had sped up to, he fled—he describes it as "running"—to Mexico City.

He wrote about this pivotal trip in an essay on his website, accompanying the release of *Witness*. Inevitable change swelled all around him. He needed to change his life, yes, but the world around him was also changing, and he suddenly felt his stagnancy in it. It was Trayvon. It was Black Lives Matter. It was his need for something to write about. And it was a potentially innocuous word like "witness"—a person who sees an event—taking on the full breadth of its meaning.

"*Witness* asks two questions I think every person in America needs to ask," he wrote. "'Am I going to be a Witness?' And in today's world, 'Is that enough?'"

> *"Am I going to be a witness? And in today's world, is that enough?"*

Booker wears a suit by Todd Snyder and stylist's own turtleneck.

> *"It would be wrong to just try to make political music, to crank it out.*
> *I've never done that, and I won't do that."*

II

Booker was born in Virginia Beach, Virginia, but moved to the outskirts of Tampa, Florida, when he was six, after his father retired from the navy. He lived with his family in a trailer park, which proved so racially hostile that they once had a cross burned on their lawn. Yet when he tells his origin story, this event is not part of it. What had a greater effect on him, he says, was being bussed 90 minutes outside of town to a school filled with predominantly white, well-to-do kids.

Despite the sometimes brutal conditions in Florida, it's where Booker got into the music and punk scenes, attending shows and skateboarding at the famous Skatepark in Tampa.

Though he'd started playing guitar at age 14, he'd yet to try anything musical in a formal capacity. He describes his relationship to the music scene then, and in college, as that of an "onlooker." He booked shows, sold merchandise and wrote about music for his college's newspaper. But he bided his time before deciding to pursue music professionally. "I don't think I had the confidence at the time to think I could play," he says.

That confidence came when he moved to New Orleans after college to work for a nonprofit that paid $800 a month—"my rent was like $500"—yet prohibited its employees from seeking outside work. In short, he needed the money. And so "Benjamin Booker" was born—quotation marks intentional. Born Benjamin Evans, Booker is a name he took on in his broke years, because of the restrictive nature of his job.

"I just put down Benjamin Booker so that if anybody saw it, they wouldn't know it was me," he says. The name Booker doesn't have a special significance for him. It doesn't represent his love of reading. It's not an homage to early civil rights activist Booker T. Washington. He thinks he may have glimpsed the name of the New Orleans musician James Booker on his way to the venue.

But to say he became a musician just to make an extra buck would be an oversimplification. Besides the pressing need for income, his decision to perform also spawned from being in a new place, where he could experiment in a low-pressure environment. "I had all of these songs that I had written for friends. So I just started doing it there. If people didn't like it, nobody knew who I was," he says. He had also come to understand that art is long and life is short. In college, he interviewed the author Chuck Klosterman, who presented him with a simple math equation: If he was spending eight hours a day at a job he didn't like, and eight hours a day sleeping, that was two-thirds of his life gone.

"He was like, 'That's bullshit. You can't waste your life.' When he told me that, that was basically the time that I started playing music," recalls Booker. Trayvon Martin's death was a jolt to the entire nation, but part of why it was so jarring to Booker was because it contradicted everything he believed about why someone could get killed. He'd grown up associating killing with gangs. Martin, an unarmed black teenager out for a walk in his suburban neighborhood, was a clear departure from that. Simply put, Booker thought: It could have been me.

A few years later, Booker was on his way to a party in New Orleans when someone started shooting—at him.

"[That's] really the reason I left New Orleans," he says. Being targeted in a world where so many other black people were being targeted, and killed, is how Benjamin Booker became a witness.

III

Since relocating to Los Angeles in 2016, Booker seems to have answered those two stirring questions about witnessing that he posed to himself, and to his listeners. In his new, far more stable life, he's found a balance between creating and living; he's returned to volunteering, something meaningful that he'd fallen out of the habit of doing.

"With the election, and all of this stuff happening, I thought, 'What can I do?' That was just something I could do. I think I really needed that. But that's why I also tell people who are freaking out, 'Just get out there.'"

Though getting directly involved with his community is important to him (his mother is a teacher, and he's passionate about education), the expectation that by virtue of having a political album means he is now an authority on politics, irks him.

"I don't think people should look to musicians as people to follow. Hopefully, [my music] makes people think about things, but I'm not an expert on anything. I'm a kid from Florida." He is adamant that he's not a gimmick and he's not a spokesperson. In fact, he makes a point in his essay of distinguishing between being a spokesperson and being a witness.

"I think that it would be wrong to just try to make political music, to crank it out. I've never done that, and I won't do that." But he is, of course, making music—he says he's been "stockpiling" songs. "Because I got into a bunch of '70s Nigerian music, and music from Ghana, I started getting into more percussion. I'm in a period of having fun. Just locked up and playing around."

"I think that now that I'm older, and I've been doing it for a little bit, I realize that I'm just… It's cheesy, but it's a musical journey," he says. "I'm working to get better at this craft—this thing that I love—and hopefully, get to a place where I'm really, really good at it."

He's reached a point where he feels comfortable in his musicianship, both where he's been, and where he's going. He quotes James Baldwin, whom he calls his "male role model" as saying, "Witness to whence I came, where I am. Witness to what I've seen and the possibilities that I think I see…."

Left: Booker wears COS head-to-toe. Right: He wears a shirt by Todd Snyder and stylist's own turtleneck.

Archive:
Valentine Schlegel

Until a few years ago, *Valentine Schlegel* had little by way of legacy: Her sculpted interiors were too immobile to be displayed in museums, and yet too domestic to be appreciated as architecture. Writer *Sarah Moroz* charts the story of a single-minded woman whose contribution to French design is only now being appreciated.

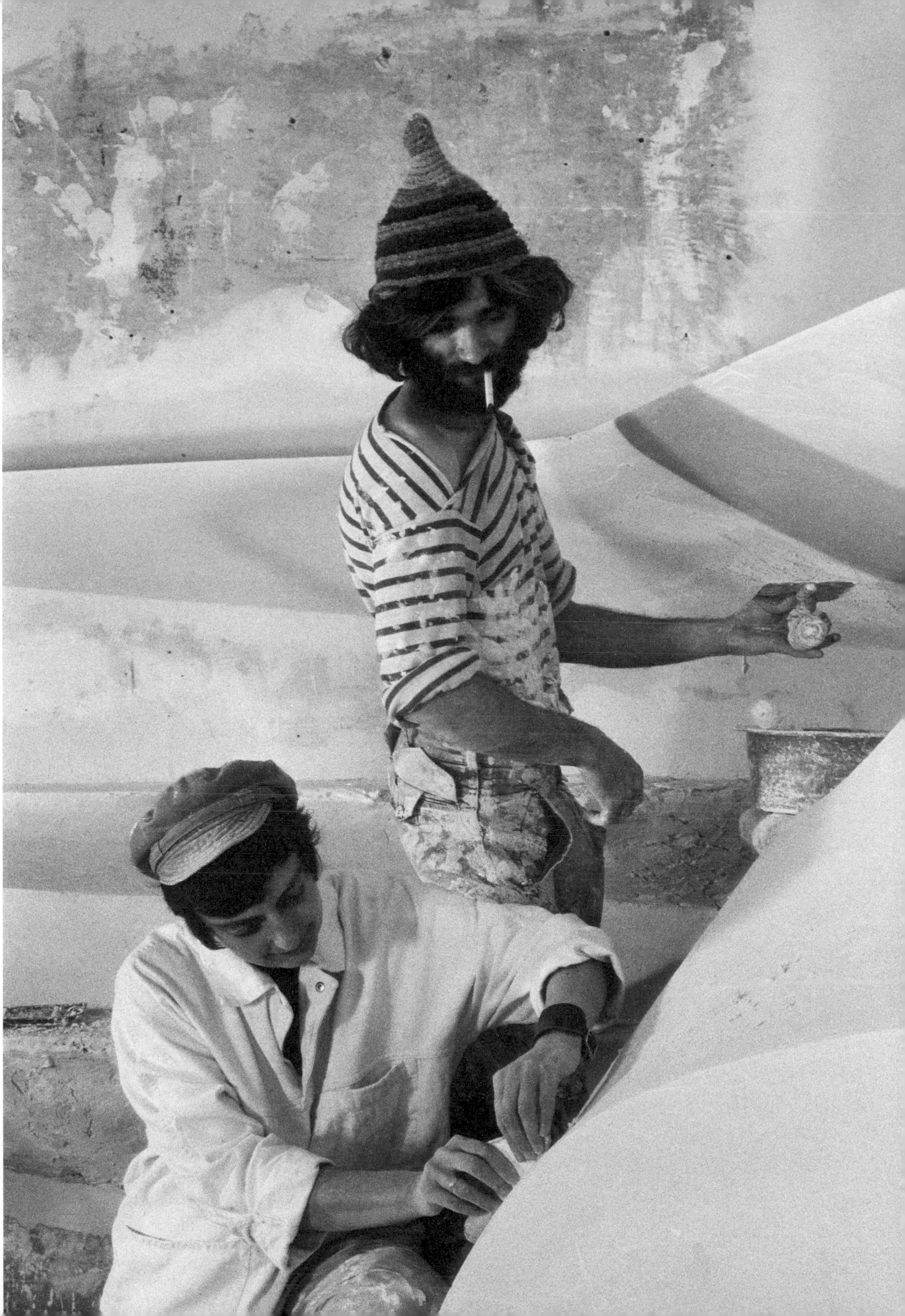

In 2017, the artist Valentine Schlegel was the subject of a long-overdue retrospective. *This Woman Could Sleep in Water,* which took place at CAC Brétigny in Paris, reintroduced one of France's most spirited and multifaceted artists to the world. The exhibition took its name from a comment made by one of Schlegel's fishermen friends, who was in awe of the sea-loving artist's ability to nap just about anywhere.

Schlegel was born in 1925 in Sète, a port city in southeastern France. Growing up in a family of artisans informed her relationship to tools and her love of the handmade. After studying drawing at the fine arts school in Montpellier, she worked for an arts festival in Avignon where she alternated between roles as a costume designer, props specialist, set painter and stage manager.

In 1945 she moved to Paris, attracted by the artistic freedoms of the cosmopolitan lifestyle and the possibility of living more comfortably as a lesbian. But the capital never outshone her tenderness for the landscapes of the south and—as her practice grew— Schlegel worked constantly with its vernacular materials and toggled between Paris and Sète. Her oeuvre drew upon her Mediterranean roots and her travels to Greece, Portugal, Spain and Italy.

After a period of experimentation, she created a series of stunning, curvaceous ceramic vases using a coil technique, mostly executed in the 1950s. The gestural contours and fantastical volumes were inspired by organic outlines of trees and birds, and evoke the freewheeling, jubilant shapes of Henri Matisse's paper cutouts. Schlegel's mastery of various crafts enabled her to make a range of everyday objects: mahogany serving utensils, a stoneware whistle shaped like a bird, painted terra-cotta figurines, leather gladiator sandals and— arguably her greatest achievement—sculptural plaster fireplaces.

Schlegel taught courses for children at the Musée des Arts Décoratifs in Paris, and it seems the process of educating went both ways: A childlike sense of playfulness is evident in many of the sculptor's designs.

Her body of work unfurled without hierarchy between milieus. Meanwhile, Schlegel also oversaw workshops for children and adolescents. She taught at Paris' Musée des Arts Décoratifs from 1958 to 1987; three of her former students, schooled in her signature pedagogy, went on to become her assistants.

Schlegel lived simply but was a bon vivant and loved preparing meals; her recipe books were dotted with bouillabaisse-style fish stew, plum tarts and apple cakes. She spent her free time gardening, cooking and sailing. And her passion for objects was intimately linked to a sense of utility; when she made an earthenware salad bowl, she delicately folded its edges inward to prevent the greens from escaping when being mixed. She maintained her marked regional accent, wore her hair in a cropped style and sported androgynous uniforms typically worn by sailors.

When living away from the south, she nostalgically recreated its sensations—referencing the limestone of the French Camargue and the undulating movement of sails from Sète's port life. The outlines of shells, seaside pebbles and plants in turn shaped her sinuous objects. Intended for everyday use, they were nonetheless guided by aesthetics. "A pot is designed to hold flowers. Without flowers, it's nothing. To have a life of its own, it must also be a sculpture," Schlegel insisted in an interview published in the catalog of one of her Paris exhibitions. She believed in creating *sculptures à vivre*: dynamic objects that possessed their own sense of folklore.

Schlegel's greatest innovation was born out of a simple frustration. When she sold a vase to friends in 1959, she placed it where she saw it best fit in their house, atop their fireplace—but she wasn't fond of the fireplace itself. And so she redesigned it to be a perfect platform for her piece—a graceful swell cast in white. The new creation was so successful that she continued making domestic fireplaces until 2002 (including one for iconic French actress Jeanne Moreau at her Faubourg Saint-Honoré home in 1968). These architectural outgrowths from the walls were made of wire armature and white plaster, undulating into custom-built shelving, benches and nooks. Schlegel described the endeavor in a 1962 television documentary about her work as "extending and energizing walls." She mused: "If I could cut my chimneys and houses from rock, I would do it." More and more friends commissioned her to make fireplaces, as did museum curators and parents of the children attending her workshops. Each made-to-measure installation could take from three weeks to two months to implement.

Her show-stopping fireplaces were impossible to circulate due to practical considerations, so Schlegel's work largely flew under the radar. The spotlight brightened only recently through the diligence of French artist Hélène Bertin, who spent five years exploring Schlegel's art practice and assembled a book and exhibition of her work. She interviewed Frédéric Sichel-Dulong, the artist's former assistant, along with her family, students and collectors; they recounted stories and

"Parisian society had little time for women using media not sanctioned as high art."

Mid-century interiors often featured exaggerated fireplaces, however the general trend was toward austere columns of exposed brick rather than curvaceous forms.

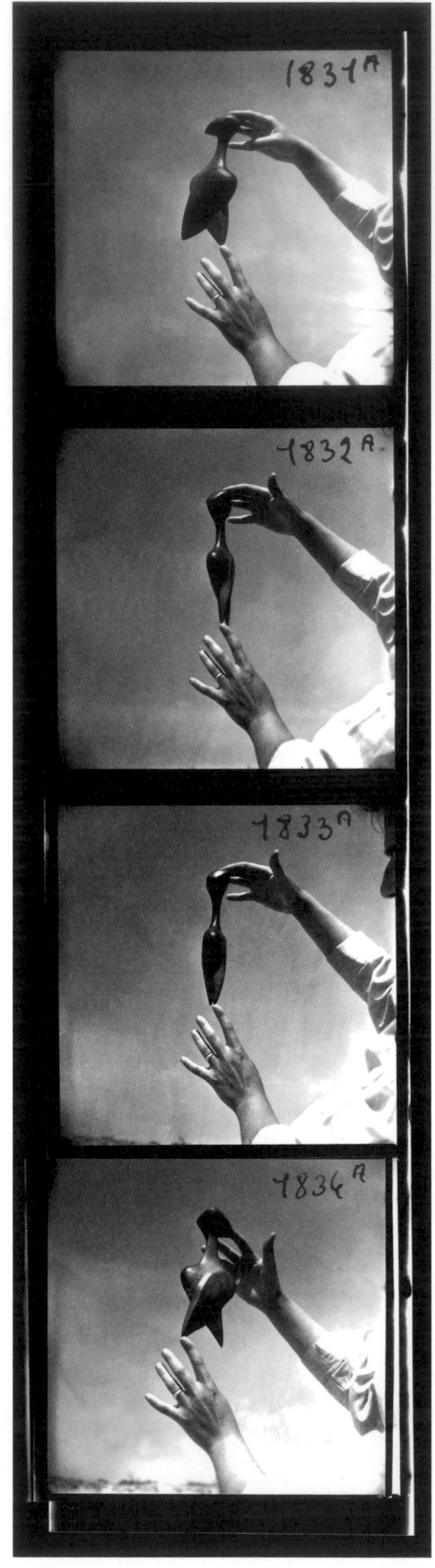

In 2017, the artist Valentine Schlegel was the subject of a long-overdue retrospective. *This Woman Could Sleep in Water*, which took place at CAC Brétigny in Paris, reintroduced one of France's most spirited and multifaceted artists to the world. The exhibition took its name from a comment made by one of Schlegel's fishermen friends, who was in awe of the sea-loving artist's ability to nap just about anywhere.

Schlegel was born in 1925 in Sète, a port city in southeastern France. Growing up in a family of artisans informed her relationship to tools and her love of the handmade. After studying drawing at the fine arts school in Montpellier, she worked for an arts festival in Avignon where she alternated between roles as a costume designer, props specialist, set painter and stage manager.

In 1945 she moved to Paris, attracted by the artistic freedoms of the cosmopolitan lifestyle and the possibility of living more comfortably as a lesbian. But the capital never outshone her tenderness for the landscapes of the south and—as her practice grew—Schlegel worked constantly with its vernacular materials and toggled between Paris and Sète. Her oeuvre drew upon her Mediterranean roots and her travels to Greece, Portugal, Spain and Italy.

After a period of experimentation, she created a series of stunning, curvaceous ceramic vases using a coil technique, mostly executed in the 1950s. The gestural contours and fantastical volumes were inspired by organic outlines of trees and birds, and evoke the freewheeling, jubilant shapes of Henri Matisse's paper cutouts. Schlegel's mastery of various crafts enabled her to make a range of everyday objects: mahogany serving utensils, a stoneware whistle shaped like a bird, painted terra-cotta figurines, leather gladiator sandals and—arguably her greatest achievement—sculptural plaster fireplaces. Her body of work unfurled without hierarchy between milieus. Meanwhile, Schlegel also oversaw workshops for children and adolescents. She taught at Paris' Musée des Arts Décoratifs from 1958 to 1987; three of her former students, schooled in her signature pedagogy, went on to become her assistants.

Schlegel lived simply but was a bon vivant and loved preparing meals; her recipe books were dotted with bouillabaisse-style fish stew, plum tarts and apple cakes. She spent her free time gardening, cooking and sailing. And her passion for objects was intimately linked to a sense of utility; when she made an earthenware salad bowl, she delicately folded its edges inward to prevent the greens from escaping when being mixed. She maintained her marked regional accent, wore her hair in a cropped style and sported androgynous uniforms typically worn by sailors.

When living away from the south, she nostalgically recreated its sensations—referencing the limestone of the French Camargue and the undulating movement of sails from Sète's port life. The outlines of shells, seaside pebbles and plants in turn shaped her sinuous objects. Intended for everyday use, they were nonetheless guided by aesthetics. "A pot is designed to hold flowers. Without flowers, it's nothing. To have a life of its own, it must also be a sculpture," Schlegel insisted in an interview published in the catalog of one of her Paris exhibitions. She believed in

3
Print

Excerpt:
Franck Durand

In *Kinfolk* co-founder Nathan Williams' forthcoming book, *The Eye, Franck Durand* explains how he is building a once-defunct *Holiday* magazine into a mini empire. Words by *Sarah Moroz* & Photography by *Lasse Fløde*

"For me, a magazine is a reality; there is a kind of tribe that goes with it."

Franck Durand, the founder and creative director of his namesake Parisian design studio, radiates a mix of boyishness and poise. He looks unassuming in a light blue turtleneck, slim white jeans frayed at the ankles and argyle socks. His brown boots are the same style he's been wearing since age 13—ditto his watch and cologne. He doesn't change what works. Although he pauses often when speaking, he doesn't lack any certainty in his stance regarding classic style, beautiful craftsmanship and metropolitan progress.

His atelier is located on rue Chabanais, a quiet side street in Paris' second arrondissement. His office features a marble-topped round table and a curated pile of books on a vintage chair (Viviane Sassen's *Pikin Slee*, Henri Matisse's *Cut-outs*). A vintage *Holiday* magazine cover (dedicated to Texas, featuring a cowboy) is propped against the wall. There's expansive white shelving, only partially filled with rows of slender red binders. His desk is a tidy arrangement of pens, a vase, glass paperweights and assorted skincare products. Everything is crisp and elegant, the surfaces nearly bare.

Durand grew up in a bourgeois family and went to a religious boarding school in Touraine. His first thrilling sense of the outside world was when a friend returned from London with the magazines *The Face* and *i-D*. "There were incredible and very different things happening elsewhere," he remembers thinking at the time. He wanted to participate.

At the age of 20, he began working for influential French art director Marc Ascoli. "There were a thousand paths that appealed to me; everything was potentially beautiful," he says. He wanted to try his hand at ceramics, work in forests, ameliorate the environment by "putting trees where there were none." He spent the latter half of his 20s working for a landscaper. "I was digging holes all day," he laughs, "but I liked it." When he became a father, he decided to set up his own design practice. The endeavor has, since its beginning in 2004, been underpinned by one main goal: "I want to put a form of beauty in everything," he says.

This approach to beauty—*le beau*—is something he has applied to many fashion campaigns, from Armani to Balmain, Chloé to Isabel Marant. "I am obsessed with what is not trendy," Durand declares. "I like the patina of things, the wear, transgenerational existence. Luxury is not profusion, or the accumulation of expensive things. It is a question of quality." Casual timelessness is not always in line with more ostentatious contemporary tastes, and he admits that: "For a person who wants to be super fashionable, super flashy, there will be no resonance in what we do." Instead, he expounds: "I'm not nostalgic at all, but I enjoy a classic; it's a form of sex appeal that I like."

This even-keeled take defies the whiplash of designer turnover. "There is the *maison*, and there is fashion," he says. "Fashion is fragile. It is important that the maison remains very solid, hard to shake." The latter provides the cornerstone for Durand's commercial vision. While Durand has been entrusted with envisaging the look of many labels, he has also been overseeing his own project. He revived *Holiday* magazine—with his accent, he pronounces it "oh-lee-deh"—a periodical originally published in America between 1946 and 1977 and presided over by a hedonistic masthead. It featured work by the greats: visuals by Henri Cartier-Bresson and Cecil Beaton, bylines from Ernest Hemingway and Colette. Durand's Frenchified update is a more self-consciously studied biannual travelogue; it is wholly lifestyle focused and abstains from politics and topical news. Jamie Hawkesworth and Inez & Vinoodh are among the contemporary contributors, and each issue spotlights a single destination (California, Denmark, South Korea, Scotland, Argentina). While the magazine sweeps the world, it has spawned a wave of extremely Parisian projects in the westerly 16th arrondissement. It's where Durand lives with his wife, Emmanuelle Alt (the editor in chief of *Vogue Paris*), and their two children. This neighborhood, dubbed Village Boileau, is "very specific and charming"—it has houses with gardens—yet Durand notes that "it almost feels abandoned." The area has no obvious draw. "It's a no-man's land, it's the Wild West. But I like this place because it just looks like nothing else in Paris. Nothing was 'done' to it, nothing has budged."

Durand decided to open a café in this "arid" sector of the metropolis in 2016. "The people who live here did not have the quality of life that went with these villas," he notes. He was strongly advised against setting up a business here by many, including his accounting team. But Durand's conviction won out. Holiday Café is housed in a building from the 1940s; it has a stark white exterior and small *terrasse*. The menu changes daily and serves traditional French fare. (As Irwin Shaw once said, "Everything in Paris starts at a café table.")

"I always thought that *Holiday* could be more than a magazine; it could be a house, a lifestyle," he muses. "Whatever we do in print would simply become an extension of that. I wanted to do a café because it would be a physical, three-dimensional experience." He notes how anything from an image to a video to a magazine is a statement on life. "For me a magazine is a reality; there is a kind of tribe that goes with it," he says. "And that's why it's good to make it exist in real life. It is the *Holiday* panoply."

That's also the case with the launch of a Holiday clothing line that Durand has developed. There are collegiate sweatshirts with "Holiday" written across the chest, tweed blazers and Shetland pullovers. Durand believes in "being really well dressed, but with no affect." He feels "inspired by older people, especially those living in the 16th arrondissement—how they mix something in a floral pattern with a Monoprix bag."

Not surprisingly, Durand continues to expand the Holiday universe. An exhibition and boutique space, housed in a building from the 1960s, joins the magazine, café and clothing label. Like the café, the space was "almost a rehabilitation project," he says: Whatever was not original was removed, so attractive structural elements, like the vitrine and facade, could be highlighted. (Durand deems the approach a "theater of decor.") "The venues are like the magazine, in a way. We wanted to preserve the essence of what once was," he says. It's also a mission he will broaden throughout the neighborhood by honoring the architecture and decor of several nearby shops. He aims to "create an ecosystem," spanning a boulangerie, an *épicerie*, a hotel and an association of *commerçants du quartier*.

"These are propositions we can make, which are convictions. It's not an aesthetic," he insists. "It's more of an attitude." Durand wishes he could do this "for a thousand other things," including urbanism; he even dreams about advising Paris city hall. Durand's project is not about citywide expansion, however, but about making the local better, the day-to-day more luxurious. "I want to shine a light on a neighborhood of forgotten Paris," he says.

Durand says he never visits the destination featured in *Holiday* before he starts an issue.

IN PRINT

For the season of change: prints and patterns as varied as the turning leaves.

Photography by *Pelle Crépin* & Styling by *David Nolan*

Xiaomeng wears a knit by Missoni, trousers by Pringle and earrings by COS. Reuben wears a knit by Missoni and trousers by Anderson & Sheppard.

Left: Xiaomeng wears a dress by Ryan Lo, socks by COS and shoes by John Lobb. Right: She wears a knit by Sonia Rykiel and trousers by Paul Smith.

A HISTORY
OF PASSPORTS

TEXT:
NEDA SEMNANI

130   PRINT

Passports grant protection. That dog-eared pamphlet whose pages are stamped with the memory of exciting experiences abroad is—for those who move through life without it—a barrier not only to travel, but to all forms of security. How did the passport become the most important piece of paper any of us will ever have? Neda Semnani charts the history of the passe-port—a document shaped by war, trade and the fear of outsiders.

On the morning of April 10, 2018, a group of nearly 150 people filed into an ornate, wood-paneled courtroom at the Prettyman Federal Courthouse in Washington, D.C. There they waited—*a little longer*, yet—to become naturalized American citizens.

Among this group was David Storey, a television news producer. Originally from Scotland, Storey moved to the United States as a 16-year-old, landing in New York as a high school exchange student. That was 24 years ago. Storey has not been back to Scotland since, at least not to live.

That morning, he was dressed smartly in a well-tailored blue suit, a crisp white button-down shirt and a striped tie. His seat was assigned in the front row, directly across from the dais where two judges would preside over a ceremony that promised to transform him into an American.

After waiting patiently in a series of lines, Storey was handed a white envelope stuffed with bureaucratic detritus, including a voter registration form, a passport application,

a copy of the oath of citizenship and a small American flag attached onto a wooden stick with glue. The morning, Storey felt, was proving anticlimactic.

"I had this vision in my head of people waving flags and judges giving uplifting speeches, but there were administrative things and grumpy court clerks," he says. "I wanted the citizenship ceremony to be, 'Here's the passport. Welcome to America.'"

The first thing that Storey did when he returned to his Brooklyn home, then, was to nip out to the post office and apply for his passport. "For me," he says, "the passport was the sign that I'm actually a citizen."

For such a small document, the passport is as complicated, fraught and powerful an object as has ever existed. For some, the booklet reads like a diary—one that we store in our bedside table, tuck away in a hotel safe or keep between our clothes and skin as we travel the world. Flipping through its pages can deliver a hit of nostalgia—each stamp conjures a memory of time spent outside our countries, perhaps even our

comfort zones. However, those same few dozen pages between a laminated cardboard cover also contain the story of the civilized world, from biblical times until the present day. Humanity's technical advances are stored within the passport.

The term *passe-port*, from the French "to pass a sea port," was first used in the 15th century. As the scholar Craig Robertson points out in his book, *The Passport in America: The History of a Document*, it had historical antecedents: An early example of papers issued for travel is written in the book of Nehemiah, from the Hebrew Bible. "If it pleases the king," the passage goes, "may I have letters... so they provide me safe conduct?"

According to Robertson, the passport wasn't really necessary throughout most of history, save for diplomatic or military reasons. Before the Industrial Revolution, the general population was mostly immobile.

A version of the passport appeared in the New World for the first time in the late 1700s. Robertson tells the story of Founding Father

Benjamin Franklin needing an official-looking way to send a congressman from his nascent nation to Holland. Franklin, ever inventive, wrote out a *passe-port* in French, which requested the congressman and his servant enjoy a safe month-long journey. He printed the page, signed it and *voilà*: The birth of the American passport.

In these early instances, the *passe-port* didn't display the citizenship or the identity of the document's holder. It was more or less taken on faith that the man named or perhaps described in the document was who he said he was, and that so too were the wife, children and servants who may have accompanied him. Special passports that included identification were only issued for people whose right to circulate freely might be questioned, including free African-Americans, divorced women and widows.

"[Modern] passports were not conceived to let people travel freely," says Atossa Araxia Abrahmian, author of *The Cosmopolites: The Coming of the Global Citizen*, which examines the buying and selling of passports, and thus citizenship, in the 21st century. "They were conceived as a way to keep people in: The idea was to account for people, to make sure they didn't go places they weren't supposed to go." States needed to make sure their citizens weren't dodging the law or the military draft.

Alphonse Bertillon, a police officer working in France during this period, was aghast at the haphazard way the state identified criminals. He developed myriad methods to identify physical traits and help officials distinguish one person from another. One lasting contribution from Bertillon is the fingerprint, a feature of many passports around the world; another is the mug shot, a version of which is the modern passport photo.

In the years between World Wars I and II, a modern bureaucracy was created around the design and issuance of the passport, and, in 1920, the first in a series of international conferences was held. The passport became a book with a standardized form, evolving from a single sheet of paper—folded in half and then in half again—into an official way for governments to track, sort and, as Robertson states, identify "the criminal, the insane, the poor, and, to a lesser extent, the immigrants."

At that time, the passport began to confer the rights and privileges of citizenship onto the person who clutched it. Within living memory, the passport—that quaint little booklet tucked in the pocket of your bag—has existed as the tactile summation of modernity's most complex issues: the rise of the nation state, international relations, racial politics, gender politics, class issues and the technical advances in policing and surveillance that have come to characterize a post-9/11 world.

Today's passport doesn't only give a person the authority to roam, it also symbolizes the right to stay put, to plant roots and declare themselves home. Indeed, perhaps one reason why only 40 percent of American citizens own a passport today is that they feel relatively secure in their nation's future, and their place within it. If that home becomes dangerous, however, the passport allows the holder to travel and to seek safe harbor elsewhere; it is also a slice of one's homeland, carrying some of its laws and protections.

In his forthcoming book, *The Design Politics of the Passport: Materiality, Immobility and Dissent*, Mahmoud Keshavarz, a design scholar based in Sweden, examines the abstract intricacies of the document.

He writes that although "a passport is frequently defined as a booklet issued by a national government that identifies the bearer as a citizen of that country, with permission to travel abroad and return under the nation's protection," it also "participates in the manipulation of the world."

He begins his treatise on the design politics of the passport with a story inverse to that of newly minted American David Storey. Keshavarz introduces us to Nemat, a 16-year-old undocumented Afghan boy living in Sweden. He and his family left Afghanistan for the first time in 2002, after they had been forced to flee the ravages of the US-led war. They traveled to Iran, becoming one family among the millions of refugees (or otherwise stateless

> "Modern passports were not conceived to let people travel freely. They were conceived as a way to keep people in: The idea was to account for people, to make sure they didn't go places they weren't supposed to go."

and undocumented people) across the globe. Nemat's family became fed up with the instability and dangers of undocumented life, and returned home after a few years. Once again, life in a conflict zone drove the family back to Iran and Nemat found himself alone in the back of a truck, passing under the noses of armed guards as he was smuggled across the border.

Keshavarz writes that the teenager decided to leave Iran once more, only this time he chose to go to Europe. Nemat wanted a passport, but he didn't want one from Afghanistan. He wanted "one that could guarantee him a place in the world, a place to live, to make, to dream." For want of a passport, Nemat began to transgress borders, moving from the Middle East to Sweden, where he lived apart from his family and worked undocumented, without access to protective welfare services.

Keshavarz argues that it is the passport—the systems that surround it and the activities it inspires—that has designed "the conditions of being, moving and residing in the world." Its power varies by country—Singapore currently has the most powerful passport in the world; its citizens can freely enter 127 countries across the globe. Afghanistan has the weakest; its citizens having free access to just five other nations: Dominica, Haiti, St. Vincent and the Grenadines, Micronesia and Ivory Coast.

Whereas some people have no passport, others have multiple. Such is the case for *The*

Cosmopolites author Abrahamian, who was born in one country to parents from another, grew up in a third nation and now lives in a fourth.

Abrahamian's parents were Iranian citizens who wanted a Canadian passport for their daughter. "My mother was really, really determined that I be born there. So she got on a plane super pregnant. She didn't know the country very well, but they didn't want me to have to deal with getting a visa every time I traveled. If I was born in Canada, I could avoid that forever," Abrahamian explains.

Along with a dual Iranian-Canadian nationality, Abrahamian is also a citizen of Switzerland and now lives in the United States. "I don't have much national identity or national pride at all," she says, but, because of the experience of her parents, she grew up acutely aware of the "discrimination and limitations tied to where your passport said you were from."

David Storey does not take his American passport for granted. "I remember the morning it came," Storey says. "I heard the mailman down in the courtyard opening the mailboxes. I knew it was there because I was tracking it online. The minute I heard the mailboxes slam shut, I ran downstairs."

For a minute, Storey stood alone in the courtyard of his Brooklyn apartment complex holding the envelope. "I was smiling from ear to ear," he says, "because I got a passport. That

was more important than anything else." When he opened the package, he flipped immediately to the page bearing his picture. His face grew warm and he felt a weight lift. He had the right to belong.

When we travel with a passport, governments track our movements. Indeed, it is how they track our existence. We don't even own our passports: The state does, and it can confiscate them as it sees fit.

Abrahamian says that some people believe that within the next decade or so the passport booklet will become obsolete—a souvenir of history. There are many governments already using biometrics, fingerprints, iris scans and facial recognition technology to identify those who belong within its borders and those who do not. It's yet another evolution of the passport, though this time without the visible touchstones of a national seal, motto and emblem.

Regardless of institutional change, the passport will continue to influence the lives of individuals. Its absence, for example, will continue to contribute to the deaths of those who do not possess one—those who will suffocate in the back of trucks or drown in the Mediterranean Sea—while its presence may save and give refuge to those who do. The passport will continue to shape our world by shoring up its boundaries and regulating the flow of human beings across them.

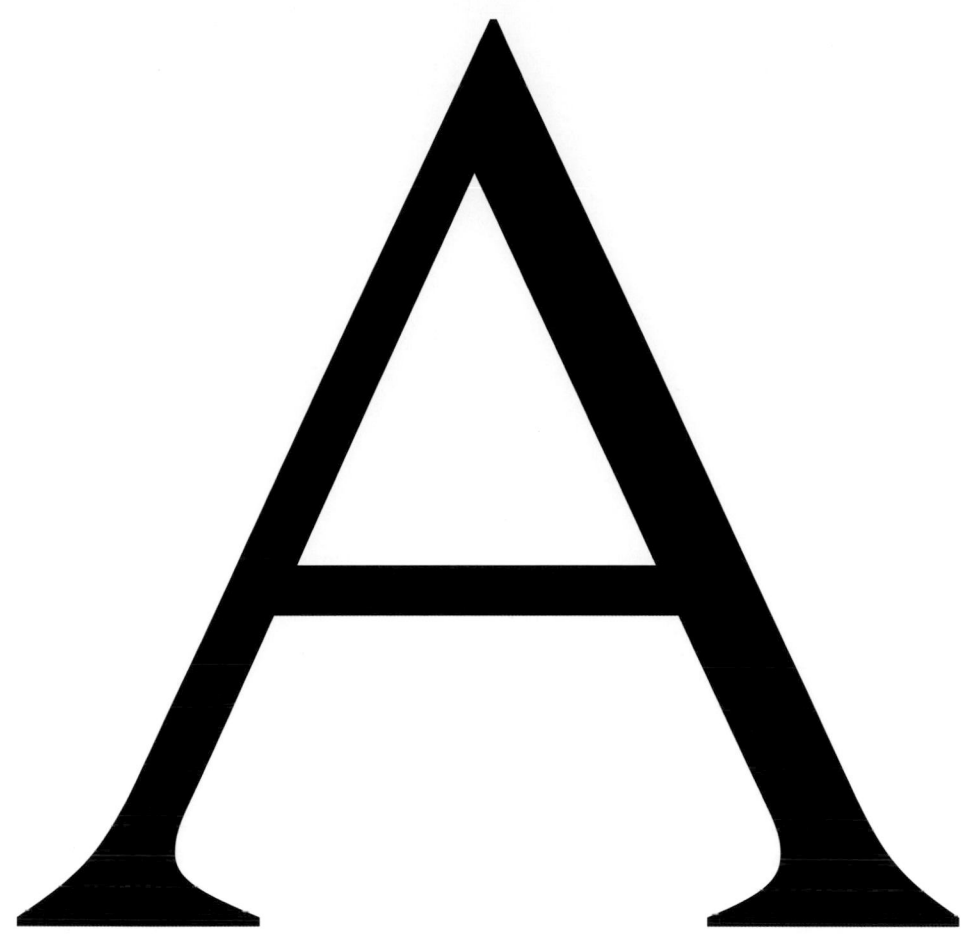

André Aciman:
Charles Shafaieh meets the Proust scholar who wrote *Call Me By Your Name*. Photography by *Christopher Ferguson*

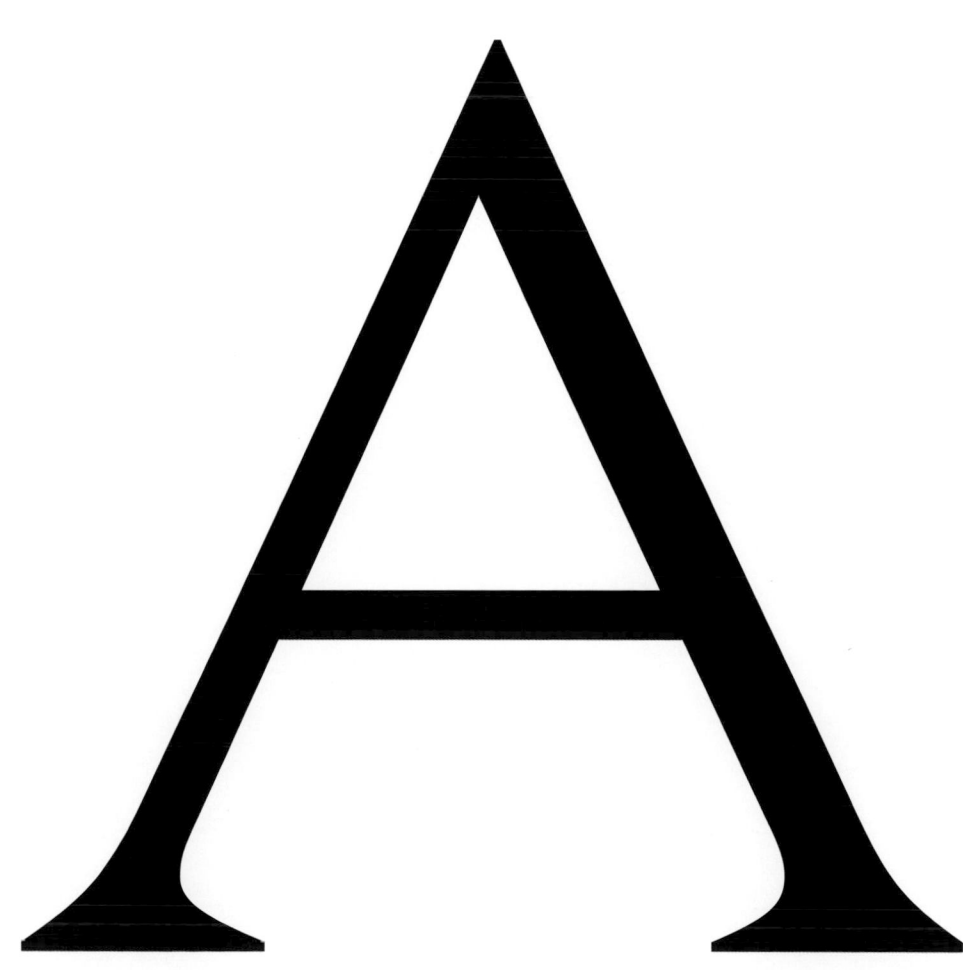

Aciman wasn't involved in the film adaptation of *Call Me By Your Name*, although he has a cameo as a man visiting the Perlman household for dinner.

André wears a coat by Deveaux, trousers by Dries Van Noten, and cardigan and shoes by Masion Margiela. Overleaf: He wears a shirt by COS and a sweater by Deveaux.

Both in conversation and through his work, André Aciman upholds writing as a serious undertaking. Being careless with words almost inevitably produces what he abhors: prose that doesn't seek to do any more than provide information.

Grasping Aciman's attention to precise diction and a sentence's cadence requires only reading a page of his many essays, his memoir of childhood in Alexandria, Egypt, or his fiction—including his 2007 debut novel, *Call Me By Your Name*, which last year was made into an Oscar-winning film.

Take this passage from *Lavender*, an essay which expands from a meditation on his father's cologne to the themes of displacement, absence, desire and longing that run through Aciman's writing: "For all I know, everything could start all over again... the life we think of each day, and the life not lived, and the life half lived, and the life we wish we'd learn to live while we still have time, and the life we want to rewrite if only we could, and the life we know remains unwritten and may never be written at all, and the life we hope others may live far better than we have..."

This refrain on groundlessness can partly be traced to past experiences. He grew up speaking French in a Sephardic Jewish family, who was pressured to leave Egypt following growing anti-Semitism after Gamal Abdel Nasser became president. In 1965, Aciman, his mother and brother moved to Rome, while his father went to Paris; they reunited and settled in New York City three years later. Now a professor of literature, Aciman didn't publish until his late thirties, following stints as a stockbroker and working in advertising.

Aciman's sensitivity for uncertainty and duality connects also with his initial urge, at age nine, toward verse. In his prose, he retains the adherence to the multiplicity of meaning engendered by poetry, which, as one character in *Call Me By Your Name* says, will "help us see double," like wine.

Thus in his intimate chamber pieces, pleasure and pain, dismissal and longing, hatred and love are bound together in his probing of the pregnant physical spaces between his characters as well as the depths within them. He captures the bliss and terror of seduction, and in doing so—like Proust, Sterne, and other writers he admires—pushes prose to new limits.

What is the writer's task? Not to have the reader discover the writer but rather himself. Great writing makes you think what the author is thinking and believe that you have come up with it yourself, whereas in fact you may never have thought those things but were always vaguely aware of them. The author articulates things in such a way as to make you believe they were yours.

That merging of two consciousnesses has an erotic quality. Erotic is a highly charged word. I prefer a fouler one: libidinous—which is at once sexual, intellectual and emotional. Writers need to open up the page to allow the reader to slip into the spaces between clauses, enmeshing you in the rhythms and cadences, so that eventually you're seduced without even being aware of it.

One of the difficulties I have as a writer who wants to read contemporary prose is that I look at the first few sentences of a new book and become horrified. And it's not just the prose's flat-footedness and the reportorial manner used to get you in right away. There's absolutely no search for deeper meaning. These writers don't do the one thing I ask of them: enchant me. I want to be taken to that magical realm where great words, put together, will make me happy—or whatever other emotion they arouse.

"The author articulates things in such a way as to make you believe they were yours."

In *Call Me By Your Name*, language, specifically the act of calling someone you feel passionately about by your name, fuses the two main characters—Elio and Oliver—in a way that bodies can never accomplish. Skin-on-skin contact is the most amazing thing. It's irreducible. But when someone with your name tells you that theirs is the same, and begins to discuss names with you, a bond is created. It's a flimsy bridge, but something exists between the two of you. Using the name a couple of times, back and forth, creates an electrifying, almost arousing, traffic.

Calling each other by the other's name displaces you entirely and makes you superconscious of yourself and the other person, and the transfer of identities becomes almost orgasmic. It might even bypass the physical connection and be more powerful. The cliché in lovemaking is that you say "I love you" even if you don't mean it, because it makes things more rhapsodic, and at that point, we realize that the words themselves carry a resonance with which even the body can't catch up with.

Elio and Oliver never tell each other "I love you." I didn't want them to! I wanted to avoid that cliché. That word—"love"—in most of my books is used in phrases like "I love fish," "I love the sunset." My characters never say it to each other because you want them to say something more powerful, like "I worship you."

Do the most enchanting words ever replace the pleasures of "real life" for you? There's absolutely no question that literature is secondary to the experience of life. My father was a great reader, but he understood reading was an escape. When he saw me reading as a young man, he would say, "Why don't you go out? Have fun, get laid! Just do something other than read books." I've internalized that and have been very lucky in that I have a life and wonderful children for whom I will forgo having anything to do with writing.

But what about the way in which art mediates life—how films now "teach us" how to kiss, for example? Literature has taught me how to read, understand and relate to people. I may be entirely wrong in how I read them, but when I question people's motives, it's because of something I've picked up from novels—particularly Dostoevsky, Stendhal and Proust. They taught me that people are not who they seem to be, that they're full of contradictions one needs to excavate, interpret and explain.

Is there anything that literature is incapable of achieving? Art is extremely important, but it's not the real thing. Real life is people, love, pleasure. A beautiful sunset never did it for me and I hate the countryside, but being on the Mediterranean in a nice house, having a wonderful dinner with people I love, makes me very happy. A page of literature doesn't do anything like that; it doesn't beat good company. Writers who believe that writing is superior to their lives offer a paradox I am unable to resolve.

Do you have any writing rituals? None. No system. No timetable. I usually write on a computer, but I find it very freeing to be on a bus or subway with a piece of paper with something already printed. Yesterday, on the way to a party, I wrote this [he picks up a printed page covered with handwritten notes]. It's all nonsense. It doesn't count and isn't serious, but it frees me to write things later that I wouldn't have thought of, because when you're typing on the computer, you're thinking, you're being "serious." But when you're dashing things off, you're not editing.

In a previous interview, you said you "had to write for America, in America"—are you succeeding? To write for America is weird because you want to maintain your own idiom, to safeguard that from the intrusion of the public and the market. People say I'm an American writer—because I've lived in America for 50 years—but I'm not an American writer, or a French or Italian writer. I speak and write notes in French and Italian, but I wouldn't dare write in either—the frame of mind of a person writing in Italian is not that of an Anglo-Saxon person.

I may be a French writer who writes French novels in English that have a Mediterranean cast. I've learned what Americans want and what I want, and they're not usually compatible. You have to meld the two in order for both voices—one voice and one expectation of a voice—to find a moment of compromise.

"Being on the Mediterranean in a nice house, having a wonderful dinner with people I love, makes me very happy. A page of literature doesn't do anything like that; it doesn't beat good company."

In a 1994 review of Aciman's memoir Out of Egypt, *The New York Times* described him as coming from a "fractious clan of dreamers and con men."

Aciman's most recent novel, *Enigma Variations*, tells the story of its main character through five loosely interconnected episodes.

"I've devoted my life to paper, and yet I'm constantly demoting and derogating it... There's nothing sacred about paper. At the end of the day, one wraps fish with paper."

A style, ultimately, is a compromise between what you might jot down in a diary and what the reader is expected to understand. You have to come up with a language that mirrors what you want to say and that will be understood, emotionally, by the reader. Style is a manufacturing, or compromise, of what your vision is.

Your cosmopolitan identity is connected, in certain ways, to the sense of homelessness and exile you experience. How does that foundation—or lack thereof—inflect your writing? You don't know where you belong partly because you can't build roots anywhere. You also don't want to make roots. I don't want to belong to America; there are many things I don't like about it. I like New York up to a certain point, but there is nowhere I like better. I like Rome and Paris, but I couldn't exist in them beyond two weeks. Ultimately, I always long for 110th Street. In *Enigma Variations*, I wrote about not wanting to be on either bank of the river but in the little island in-between that doesn't exist.

The place I live is on paper—but then I call one of my essay collections *False Papers*, as if to undercut whatever presumption there is that a writer can live his whole life in books. That's why my other essay collection is called *Alibis*: You don't belong anywhere, just alibis of places. I don't belong in the 21st or 20th centuries, and I certainly don't belong in 4th-century BC Athens. I don't know where I stand nationally, sexually, religiously. They're all mobile. I write about this as a plea to resolve it in one way or another, but I'm unable to. I don't know how. I don't know where I belong. Or who I am.

I do know that I cannot deal with people who are totally French or American—people who are fully immersed in their culture. I need people who are slightly off, slightly unhinged, interested in something else. If you're just one thing alone, I can't deal with you.

The Italian philosopher Antonio Gramsci wrote that a person is "a product of the historical processes to date, which has deposited in [them] an infinity of traces, without leaving an inventory." Is your writing a constant attempt to compile that inventory? I'm very careful about this because, on one hand, the attempt to find ligatures between X, Y, and Z and create a kind of narrative around them is the compulsion to write. But you have to be distrustful of writing's power to create

this sense of order—again *False Papers*. Paper will automatically want to create order, symmetry, harmony and meaning. You have to distrust that about paper. There's no order. I always end up untying what I have tied up because I don't trust it. Paper will always try to bring you home, but I will remain rootless and eradicated forever.

Is your fiction also imbued with this archeological project and its paradoxes? Or are you writing as a means of distancing yourself from the past? You don't know whether you're writing to see better or in order not to see at all—to stop seeing.

When writing about the past—as in my memoir and my fiction—you're trying to resolve or repossess the past, to take hold of it so you can say, "Now you're in my pages." It's not true though, because why am I then writing another essay about the past or about being elsewhere? I haven't solved it yet. I don't think I can. I keep writing because I'm still trying to come up with the right key, so I write the same book with a different plot, voice, characters.

Writing is allegedly the means of burying the past. But the next thing you know, it just comes back up. It's like writing a book about somebody you loved very passionately. Sure enough, you wake up one morning, after you thought that book got rid of them, and you're in love with them again. Possessing and dispossessing are the same gesture.

I'm writing an essay now that I've written many times before. I rewrite it because the resolutions promised by writing give me the slip each time. I'm trying to ground myself in time or place, or even on paper, and yet find that the very devices that allow me to do so are the very ones that undo what I'm attempting to do. That's why I think I'm a pure ironist, because everything I do is already being undercut. As I'm writing a sentence, I'm already rewriting it before I've even finished it.

That awareness of the task's impossibility is always there, but you're still going to keep at it in whatever manner you can. I've devoted my life to paper, and yet I'm constantly demoting and derogating it. I refuse to take it seriously, because of my father's injunction: "Don't keep writing all the time—go out and get laid!" If I lie in my writing, so what? If I've changed a few things, who is to know and who cares? There's nothing sacred about paper. At the end of the day, one wraps fish with paper.

At Work With:
Nicolas Ouchenir

Gossip columnists can only dream of possessing the high-society access pass handed to *Nicolas Ouchenir* by virtue of his unusual talent. As the go-to calligrapher for many fashion houses, he is personally responsible for penning over 15,000 invitations every Fashion Week—and he's made his mark on the tattoos, trees and even gravestones of various wealthy clients. *Pip Usher* meets the man with the golden hand. Photography by *Marsý Hild Þórsdóttir*

Nicolas Ouchenir calls from the Cannes Film Festival and switches his phone to video mode so that a panorama of the Mediterranean before him can be appreciated. He is seated at a long table that has been laid for a lavish lunch. Giddily, he zooms the camera in on a place card scrawled in the elegant calligraphy that has made him France's go-to man for all manners of correspondence. "Penelope Cruz," it reads.

When the camera resumes focus on his face, he's grinning. "It's a good life," he says, glancing at the brilliant sunshine and spectacular views afforded from the terrace. Calligraphy—deriving from the Greek words *kallos* (beauty) and *graphein* (to write)—has long been an esteemed art form and Ouchenir, who counts Christian Dior Couture, Chloé, Chanel and many more of the world's most storied fashion houses as clients, has built an illustrious career from his command of the fountain pen. After 15 years, it seems the novelty of corresponding with the fashionable and famous as Paris' most sought-after calligrapher has yet to wear off.

Ouchenir is quick to note, however, that he's not summoned to these gilded events to play. Instead, "it's only meetings and writing." Therein lies the curious paradox of his profession. On the one hand, Ouchenir is a gatekeeper of the city's secrets; his handwritten invitations chronicle who commands power in a world that permits entry to very few. "My work allows me to be inside Paris at large," he says. "I know who becomes persona non grata, who divorces, who is the mistress of whom. I know the access codes of each person's door. Obviously, it's intriguing but people trust me." On the other hand, he is personally responsible for penning more than 15,000 invitations (and their envelopes) each Fashion Week, a grueling task that requires his right hand—insured for a figure he will only admit to being "super expensive"—to be in pristine condition. The hours can be grueling, the work painstaking and repetitive, and the requests, well, occasionally rather unexpected.

"I could use anything as a tool... A few years ago, someone called me to write with pig's blood."

In daily life, writing by hand is becoming increasingly uncommon. Calligraphy, however, is enjoying the opposite trajectory; the more online communication comes to dominate, the more clients come to value a personal touch.

HOW TO SIGN OFF

by Pip Usher

How do you see yourself? Are you sympathetic and accommodating (in which case cursive in a gentle slope should relay that well) or does the spikiness of your temperament show through the jagged peaks of your scrawl? According to Ouchenir, a signature holds the key to one's character; it allows us to "see the rhythm and the sensitivity of a person." If you're suddenly panicked by the chicken-scratch of your own sign-off, remember that the whole point is that it's supposed to reflect you. Ouchenir offers reassurance in the insistence that his own signature was an organic development rather than a studied exercise in self-reflection. "The principle of a signature is not to be able to explain it," he says. (Top: Opéra deckle-edge writing set by G. Lalo, Center: Ocean green ink bottle by Graf Von Faber-Castell, Bottom: Desk fountain pen by ystudio.)

"Last time I was in Moscow they asked me to engrave a tombstone in a cemetery," he says of a commission that found him carving an epitaph in the cold, gray depths of a Russian winter. "It was like a horror movie," he continues, and then shrugs. "It was weird but well-paid—sometimes you have to do that." Another client in Palm Springs admired his work so much that they paid him to etch into their trees. "So there's a garden of Nicolas Ouchenir calligraphy," he exclaims, tickled at the thought. There are also the bespoke tattoos that decorate the skin of those with enough money to pay for them—another request that, Ouchenir admits, he still finds a little peculiar.

Born to a French mother and an Algerian father in the lively Parisian neighborhood of Belleville, Ouchenir grew up in a rich stew of cultural and religious influences. "All the religious texts—the Torah, the Bible, the Quran—were at our schools," he says. Such exposure may explain the origins of his talent: Islamic calligraphy is a highly venerated tradition with a range of styles (angular strokes, flowery scripts, decorative flourishes), while biblical texts penned in Europe tend to favor more functional forms. As a child, he remembers being entranced by a drawing that depicted Moses' Crossing of the Red Sea. "It was a drawing just with lines—no letters, just lines of ink," he says. "Even when I was young, this kind of drawing appealed."

Later, while working a gallery job, Ouchenir discovered the considerable power of a handsomely handwritten note for himself. Assigned the task of inviting prospective clients to an event, he took a bottle of wine down to the gallery's basement and began to play around. The invitations were a success—more than 100 guests showed up. It was his first inkling that, in an age of throwaway emails and mass messages, the rarity of personalized correspondence yields results.

When a close friend died, Ouchenir decided to leave Paris behind for a trip to "the end of the world." The reality was 18 months in São Paulo, which he spent working as a production assistant for *Vogue Brasil*—a demanding role that required ample time on planes and at parties. Just as burnout loomed, the call came. "I need your handwriting," pleaded a collector from his gallery days. Ouchenir was soon on a plane back to Paris with a commission to handle the calligraphy and correspondence for a banquet thrown by the American Friends of Versailles.

In the years since, life has been anything but pedestrian. "I love doing new stuff," he says, "I love to be afraid and I hate when things are mundane." In the overbooked crush of Fashion Week, when each fashion house is vying for the patronage of influential editors and famous faces in their front row, Ouchenir's handwritten invitations have become de rigueur for designers hoping to distinguish themselves. "When I first met Monsieur Yves Saint Laurent, it was emotional; we talked a lot about my calligraphy," he recalls. Ask him about Miuccia Prada and he'll tell you that she prefers a new calligraphy each season. Rick Owens? A stickler for continuity. He admires Karl Lagerfeld's commitment to craftsmanship and the questioning mindset of Chloé.

Ouchenir's toolbox includes a hand-carved calame bamboo reed pen and a variety of fountain and automatic pens. But the materials are secondary to the idea and execution itself. "I could use anything as a tool," he shrugs. "For instance, a few years ago, someone called me to write with pig's blood."

Calligraphy is a solitary art form, but Ouchenir's atelier near the Champs-Élysées is usually a boisterous space. Music plays, acquaintances pass by with their children or their pets. Each morning, he practices calligraphy; evenings are reserved for drawing. Likening his discipline to that of a dancer, Ouchenir says that his craft demands that he remain creatively limber. Dancers find new form, he searches for new signatures. Inspiration can strike anytime—like several days prior, when he'd been dancing in a Milanese club. "Poof! Suddenly I knew what to do with the signature of this new perfume brand," he says.

"Calligraphy is how you sign yourself with your own feelings," he adds. "Nowadays, people don't write anymore because they don't know their own feelings. You have to take the pencil to make your feelings happen. It's an emotional process much more than a spiritual one. It's like an engraving of your soul."

For a man still taken with the novelty of his craft, the year ahead promises to be richly varied. There's a signet ring collaboration with French jeweler Arthus-Bertrand; a film with Pete Doherty, slated to debut at the Toronto Film Festival; two exhibitions that will open in Estonia and New York; and artwork to adorn the interiors of famed architect and designer Jacques Garcia's new château. All this, in addition to his usual fashion responsibilities, will leave little time for much else.

He isn't complaining, though. Ouchenir's "obsession and passion" for calligraphy fits within an age-old lineage of artists and scholars who have all sought to capture something profound with the strokes of their pen. "Handwriting shows candor, truth and emotion," he says. "Without handwriting, humanity is dead."

"Calligraphy is how you sign yourself with your own feelings... It's like an engraving of your soul."

Ouchenir has compared his talent to that of a dancer; everyone can dance, but only a few can do so with the grace required to perform on stage.

CLIPPINGS

In boxes, under beds and at the back of drawers; scraps salvaged from the past hold potent memories.

Photography & Styling by *Christian Møller Andersen*

217

Reflecting on her habit of painting only fragments of objects, Georgia O'Keeffe commented, "It seemed to make my statement as well or better than the whole could."

A reasoning's puzzle
in the mosaic leaves
spinning memory frames
beneath my feet;
bright yellow,
dark brown
and green;
paper-thin
and not yet to be seen.
... my canvas landscape
Fall and wonders
draw abstracts

III

157

Sifting through a box of keepsakes is an exercise in archeology. The further we dig, the deeper the memories that resurface—through letters, receipts and recipes written hastily on envelopes.

the free bird
another breeze. An
winds soft through
sighing trees. and
waiting on a da

THE SECRET LIVES OF BOOKSHELVES

TEXT: LYDIA PYNE

Playwright Alan Bennett was always frustrated by the commonplace encyclopedias that set designers used to illustrate the presence of bookshelves in his plays. "A bookshelf is as particular to its owner as are his or her clothes," he complained. "A personality is stamped on a library just as a shoe is shaped by the foot." But what aspects of our personalities do our bookshelves actually reveal? In the following excerpt from Bookshelf, Lydia Pyne climbs ladders and studies spines to find out.

The Roman poet Marcus Tullius Cicero had a serious thing for books. For Cicero, books were more than just physical texts full of abstract ideas—books were objects that imbued their surroundings with metaphysical meaning. "A room without books," Cicero famously, if somewhat apocryphally, declared, "is a body without a soul."

As a stalwart book collector in the first century BC, Cicero maintained several extensive personal libraries at his country estates as well as a library in his villa on the Palatine Hill in the center of Rome, near the Forum Romanum and the Circus Maximus. For many of Cicero's affluent colleagues, the mere show of books was enough to cement their elite, educated status in Roman society. The architect Vitruvius, Cicero's contemporary, noted, "Among cold baths and hot baths a library is equipped as a necessary ornament of a great house." Cicero's libraries, however, weren't merely the fodder of fashionable display; these libraries were rooms to be read and re-read. For Cicero, the search for truth, enlightenment, and progress rested on the knowledge that was between a book's covers—or at least between the scroll's sticks. With hundreds of volumes in his personal libraries, Cicero needed a way to organize his collection. To give a room soul, he reasoned, you would have to put books in it, but logic begged the question of where.

History tells us that we put books on a shelf. Cicero and his library suggest, however, that books don't go on just any shelf; books ought to be shelved on a proper bookshelf. What makes a bookshelf a bookshelf isn't a given thing. Every bookshelf has its own unique life history; every bookshelf speaks to its own cultural context. Bookshelves are dynamic, iterative objects that cue us to the social values we place on books and how we think books ought to be read. What makes a bookshelf a bookshelf are the recurring decisions made about its structure, architecture, and function.

Bookshelves serve as powerful symbols because they have a particularly powerful cultural cachet that connotes specific expectations for how we "ought" to interact with them as objects. Bookshelves immediately cue us to how we ought to interact with a room and how much importance or power we assign it. These expectations—these cues—are picked up and reaffirmed as essentially stage directions where the bookshelf serves as a prop, a MacGuffin, or even a plot device. Few, if any, other objects carry such cultural distinction and expectations in print and film. For thousands of years, books and their shelves (or, even, scrolls and their shelves) have implied access to knowledge. With this access comes everything associated with it—power and privilege. But what's most intriguing is the longevity and staying power that bookshelves have maintained.

How we portray bookshelves in fiction is actually a very telling cultural barometer of the value that we assign to them. Even in the face of their cultural extinction—or, more accurately, their imagined extinction—bookshelves offer an interpretation and argument about where we think our culture is going.

"What constitutes a book or a bookshelf depends, like so many things, on definition," notes Henry Petroski in *The Book on the Bookshelf*. "And that definition can change with time... Just as we may wonder if a tree makes a sound when it falls out of earshot, so we may ask, is an empty bookshelf an oxymoron?" Decisions about a shelf's structure, architecture, and function morph the thing we call a bookshelf and shape how the shelf interacts with its books. The decisions show the give-and-take of cultural mores that is inherent in every bookshelf.

How to read a bookshelf

Once books are on a bookshelf, then what? As it turns out, the life of the book on the bookshelf only begins with the categorizing of the book—just the first stage of the life cycle of the book on the shelf.

In 2014, author Phyllis Rose explored this question by reading an entire bookshelf full of fiction, left to right, in the shelf's entirety. In the introduction to her memoir-critique of the experience, *The Shelf: From LEQ to LES, Adventures in Extreme Reading*, she explains, "Believing that literary critics wrongly favor the famous and canonical—that is, writers chosen for us by others—I wanted to sample, more democratically, the actual ground of literature... I chose a fiction shelf in the New York Society Library somewhat at random—it happens to be the LEQ-LES shelf—and set out to read my way through it."

If the shelf is the organizing object for the book—literally and metaphorically—then it begs the question of what was on it. One of the most captivating observations that Rose offers is the realization that her experiment—

that she, personally—had an effect on what was kept on the shelf and for how long. The books on shelves are not inert bodies, but objects in motion (however slow that motion might be), that depend on the library's circulatory system.

This idea that a set of books on a particular shelf is a living, changing entity was reinforced through my (very informal) experiment at the local branch of the Austin Public Library. I stopped by the shelf that would hold LEQ-LES and noticed a couple of things. First, there wasn't a shelf that held the same set of books; LEQ-LES was spread out over three shelves. Secondly, I was shocked to find that there wasn't a single shared book between Rose's LEQ-LES shelf and the shelf at the Austin Public Library. The books she read were nowhere to be found on the Austin shelves. Even with the same cataloging system for books in play, where books "ought" to be on a particular shelf, there was nothing between the two sets of books on their bookshelves that overlapped. Each shelf—that combination of books and bookshelf—exists as its own, unique object, shaped by the decisions of its own library and audiences.

To some bibliophiles, books are grouped together on a shelf because they simply "go together" as some Jungian-like test of personality and psyche. Perhaps these books that "go together" were read in a particular phase of life, perhaps the books are simply the same size. For some, the books are shelved "properly"—vertically with the spines facing out; for others, some books are stored horizontally, to act as a bookend.

Statistician Nate Silver is best known for his FiveThirtyEight blog, but his arrangement of

books in his New York apartment (as featured on the blog) shows that he arranges his books by color—all of the white books occupy the top shelves, then the reds, then the oranges, moving his way through the color spectrum, finishing with the black books down near the floor.

"The books in my office—I have about 500—are arranged by color. It's quite aesthetically pleasing. It's not all that convenient, however, when I have to track down a book. I have to remember its color, or I have to scan through every row and column of the shelf. The color-coding system is perhaps a little better as an organizational method than shelving the books at random, but not a lot better. Still, with 500 books, it's a manageable problem. In the worst case, I might spend a few minutes looking for a book. I'm willing to make that trade in exchange for having a prettier bookshelf."

Any system of organizing books creates an order and an expectation; any system of putting books on a bookshelf is a trade-off between a formal catalog, security of the books, and accessibility to the books themselves. In order to find and locate a particular book or text, a system creates an expectancy that the book will appear at its appointed place in that system. In other words, how books are cataloged, shelved, and displayed shows a certain worldview and a particular system of thinking—aesthetic, pragmatic, categorical, or out-and-out haphazard, even. Regardless of underlying organizing schema, how books are displayed is a physical expression of each type of cataloging. And this means that not every subject category that groups a set of books together is going to be immediately obvious to a person looking at that bookshelf.

> "What makes a bookshelf a bookshelf isn't a given thing. Every bookshelf has its own unique life history; every bookshelf speaks to its own cultural context. Bookshelves are dynamic, iterative objects that cue us to the social values we place on books."

Cicero's shelves

For Cicero and his fellow Romans, personal libraries were ongoing building projects. While public libraries, like the Library of Celsus in present-day Turkey, were part of broader Roman culture, the private library dominated the circles of the intellectual elite and economically affluent. In the public libraries of Rome, the papyrus scroll remained the primary medium of book publication and scrolls lay open on shelves in the library storerooms with parchment labels hanging from the scrolls' wooden rollers. For private libraries, however, the Roman philosopher Seneca sniffed at the person "who seek[s] to have book-cases of citrus-wood and ivory, who collect[s] the works of unknown or discredited authors and sits yawning in the midst of so many thousand books, who gets most of his pleasure from the outsides of volumes and their titles." Seneca counseled his readers to "let just as many books be acquired as are enough, but none for mere show." As personal *bibliothecas* grew, the architectural space allotted to the library within a family's villa was frequently renovated, often decorated with images of authors, philosophers, family members, or friends.

By the turn of the first century BC, Cicero's libraries had reached a critical mass of texts and were in dire need of an upgraded shelving system. Once Cicero decided that he needed bookshelves for his burgeoning collection of books, he wrote to his friend Atticus to secure someone to build them: "I wish you could send me any two fellows out of your library, for Tyrannio to make use of as pasters, and assistant in other matters. Remind them to bring some vellum with them to make those titles." Atticus was a wealthy banker, editor, and patron of letters, and Tyrannio was an educated Greek, captured by Lucullus and brought to the Roman Republic in 72 BC. Tyrannio was employed by several wealthy Romans, including Atticus, to arrange their libraries. Atticus loaned Cicero Tyrannio and two of his assistants to help Cicero build bookshelves.

"Your men have made my library gay with their carpentry work," Cicero reported. "Nothing could look neater than those shelves of yours, since they smartened up my books with their titles." In Cicero's final letter to Atticus on the subject of his library, Cicero sings the praises of the bookshelf project, "Now that Tyrannio has arranged my books, a new spirit has been infused into my house. In this matter the help of your men Dionysius and Menophilus [the men Atticus lent to Cicero] has been invaluable... It is prodigious." We can only assume that with such remarkable bookshelves, Cicero's rooms were filled with a lot of soul.

In our everyday interactions with bookshelves, it's easy to just take them at face value—they're simply shelves for books; the stuff of libraries and offices, the bane of the mover's existence. ("Lift with your legs, not with your back.") Today we expect bookshelves to be those vertical pieces of furniture, with shelves running horizontally, storing books from top to bottom, reading left to right; we assume that books will be vertically situated with their spines facing out, displayed and cataloged in a predictable way. All of these expectations about the form and function of a bookshelf, however, are choices that have been made over and over.

Deciding to curate books. Deciding to organize those books. Deciding on a system to store and display books. Bookshelves beg the question of whether they are defined simply by their architectural design or by their use. Esoterically, we could describe the bookshelf as a linear plane, grouping together different categories of knowledge. Pragmatically, what books are put where and on which shelves reflects a particular worldview. Every shelf reflects this worldview and order, whether it's the subject-based Dewey Decimal System in "the stacks," an ordering of books by color, or the haphazardness of a toddler arranging picture books by shape.

In short, the bookshelf is how and where we create categories of knowledge and experience. Even with the advent of digital books, the bookshelf has become a visual metaphor as we add book bytes to a virtual shelf on our tablet screen; even where a bookshelf lacks physical materiality, its function endures. What a bookshelf is depends on the agency and choices of people interacting with it. These decisions swirl around the shelf and shape what it looks like and how it behaves. Everyone who cares about books cares about bookshelves. The very act of picking up a book and reading it—even perusing through it—engages a person with the book-to-bookshelf dialectic. The book had to come from a bookshelf of some sort—a bookstore, a library, a Kindle.

To put words in Freud's mouth: sometimes a shelf is just a shelf. Which might be true, at least until you put a book on it.

—

This article is an abridged and edited excerpt from Bookshelf (Object Lessons, Bloomsbury Academic)

In the age of digital everything, the currency of printed matter is appreciating. Photography by *Gustav Almestål*

PRINT:
On Money
At Libraries
In Diaries
For Posterity

Making Money

When Snøhetta decided to submit designs for Norway's new range of banknotes, the agency embarked on a journey to understand not only the technical requirements of branding a currency, but also how a banknote could be the symbol of a nation. Here, Snøhetta partner Martin Gran discusses creating the "business card of a nation," and how our collective social contract has imbued bits of colored paper with a value that far outweighs their material worth.

You designed a new currency in an era of digital payments. Were you conscious that you were making something that might soon not exist? We had a long debate about it—whether this will be the last analog money designed in Norway. We eventually concluded that this design may not be the last, because the economic institution of money is too important for digital to totally take over. You need a tangible symbol to give authority to this institution.

The new banknotes look distinctly modern. How did you go about creating something contemporary while also referencing historical precedents? We tried to link our design to history by look-ing into the first graphic representations, which we found were mosaics. This gave us a spring-board to look into the modern version of the mosaic—pixels. The concept behind the currency is called the "beauty of the boundaries"; life grows in the boundaries between land and mountains, sea and land. The bridge between heritage and modern times is also a boundary. That led to us finding a boundary between a mathematical, pixelated design and an organic pattern on top.

Did you consider the fact that you were creating a piece of national art? You could call the banknote the business card of a nation. Initially, we felt a responsibility to design something people would like. But we threw that out quickly, because the minute you start to think about what people would like, you compromise. We wanted to make a design we believed in, so we started to think about what would represent modern Norway. To be honest, we thought we would never win the competition, and that we had taken it too far. How much more of a conservative client can you get than a central bank? We have to honor the bank for daring to select our design.

In technical terms, what makes a piece of printed paper into a banknote? Before we started designing, we were invited to attend a seminar about the security measures we'd need to consider. There are about five of these. For example, when you put a banknote into a photocopier or scanner, the machine will stop. All such machines and software packages have to be licensed to recognize that pattern, which means that it's secure and that you can trust the organization behind it. Understanding that this simple piece of designed paper represents an enormously important social institution was interesting.

What does a collector look for in a banknote? For collectors, it's about uniqueness—if the design of the currency is limited or misprint-ed. With our note, there aren't many similar designs so that's an attraction. At Snøhetta, we strongly believe that our projects should influence social interactions. It occurred to us that this very small design—this piece of paper that you can fit into your pocket—may be the most social product we've done, even compared to our Oslo Opera House, because banknotes will shift through so many hands.

Words by Pip Usher

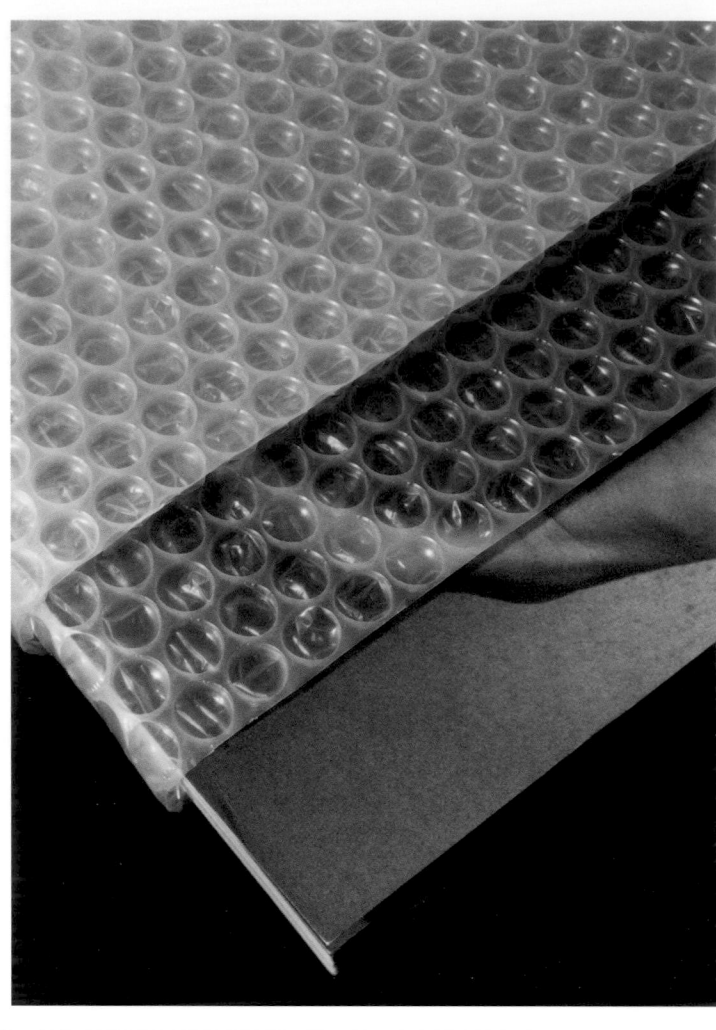

Primary Sources

Have you ever wondered what specific kind of apple tempted Eve? For one New Yorker in 1956, it was a question that plagued them enough to call up the library to find out. In a box of old reference questions discovered by the New York Public Library, the breadth—and bizarreness—of human query was revealed in a number of handwritten notes documented by staff. Some of the calls are particular to their era: One caller in 1947 inquired after the physical characteristics of Adolf Hitler. "I think I've found him," they said. "He walks heavier on one foot and everything." Others are timeless concerns, like the "somewhat uncertain" woman in 1967 who wanted to discreetly track down the identity of a fellow she knew to be worth $27 million.

In a pre-digital age, knowledge was found in two places: encyclopedias and libraries. As the gatekeepers of both, librarians often found themselves employed as human search engines by curious patrons. And back in the days before we could do a quick Google search, finding answers required trawling through aisles of books.

Even with the advent of smartphones, the New York Public Library still offers a helpline where a team of 10 librarians tries to answer any inquiry. The helpline receives more than 30,000 calls annually, with topics covering everything from social etiquette to the life cycle of lobsters.

With some questions, though, it's hard to know if the librarian managed to provide a satisfactory answer. One inquisitive art-lover in 1976 called to ask: "Why do 18th-century English paintings have so many squirrels in them, and how did they tame them so they wouldn't bite the painter?"

A notebook can play many roles. It can be a home for important information, a tool for keeping track of responsibilities or a nonjudgmental space in which to express the most shameful of feelings. This last use is arguably the notebook's most revolutionary function: It's easy to forget that we haven't always had the ability to pick up a pen and jot down observations personally important to us.

In fact, it has taken centuries for the notebook to become the distinctly individual possession that it is today. In his book *Writing the Self*, historian Peter Heehs draws a parallel between the evolution of the concept of the self and the rise of self-expression through first-person writing. Heehs reminds us that "over the last two millennia, the prevailing idea of the self has changed from a ghostly spirit to a substantial soul to an autonomous individual." Before this collective realization, there was no need for blank pages where individuals could articulate themselves privately through the written word.

The Protestant Reformation of the 16th century was a major catalyst for mass self-reflection on paper: When going to confession became a thing of the Catholic past, Protestant churches in England encouraged their followers to self-examine by keeping a diary. Eight hundred years prior, in Japan, *nikki bungaku*, or "diary literature," chronicled daily activity at the royal court, but did not reveal any personal input from the diarist. It seems that one of the first "real" bound diaries may have been the 10th-century account of a courtly Japanese lady known as Mother of Michitsuna. She lamented, in writing, that "unhappiness was part of my inescapable destiny, determined from former lives, and must be accepted as such."

As an extension of the human mind, the notebook was the precursor to the computer. Several recent studies have found that conscious journaling improves both mental and physical health. The exploding popularity of bullet journals—used to track health, habits and personal goals—corroborates this kind of research. And though many platforms for online digital diaries have been popping up recently, nothing can replace the comforting weight of the physical notebook. Even so, Heehs observes, "We've been scratching and painting and inscribing marks and lines and letters on stones and walls and papers for tens of thousands of years... But some of us have grabbed whatever tool came to hand and used it to express—or to create— ourselves." The tools may change with time, but the history of this creative form of self-expression is far from over.

Notes to Self

Words by Alia Gilbert

Words by Pip Usher

Nose Deep

Crack open the weathered pages of an old book and what do you smell? According to research conducted by Matija Strlič and his team at University College London's Institute of Sustainable Heritage, it's likely to be "a combination of grassy notes with a tang of acids and a hint of vanilla over an underlying mustiness."

It's also likely that you'll find the scent to be comforting, familiar, perhaps laced with nostalgia. Olfaction is linked directly to the limbic part of the brain responsible for memory and emotions so, when such an odor-evoked emotion surfaces, it's because your brain has been triggered to summon childhood memories. But this scent taps into a larger collective memory that we share, says Cecilia Bembibre, a PhD student who worked with Strlič to analyze, document and archive the role of historic smells in our cultural heritage. "If we want to talk about the way we lived, would we use the smell of books as entryways into who we were and what we valued?" she asks.

While buildings and objects have long been considered essential components of our heritage, the more intangible concept of scent has been largely overlooked. Yet Bembibre notes that the smell of old books has always possessed cultural clout, judging by the many quotes in literature about their musk—and the fact that brands such as Byredo are introducing book-scented candles, perfumes and oils. It may be simply that our lack of language skills around scent has prevented us from preserving it. "Because we don't have formal education on smells most of the time, it's quite hard to talk about them and describe them in a way that is standardized," she says. "Sometimes you perceive a smell and the first thing you want to say about it is a very personal memory like, 'It smells like my grandmother's purse.'"

In their quest to change this, the team at UCL worked to create a historic book odor wheel that represents the first step toward doc-umenting heritage smells. While Strlič looked at the volatile organic compounds that are off-gassed from the paper of old books, Bembibre focused on decoding the human experience surrounding the scent. Sometimes, she'd take groups of people to the library and ask them to describe the aromas—"woody" and "musty" were commonly used as people gazed around at the heavy wooden furniture and dusty tomes. In another study, she presented an unlabeled canister containing the scent and asked people to detail what they smelled without any visual cues. This time, they mentioned notes of chocolate, cocoa, coffee and vanilla.

"At a point when our personal libraries are getting smaller and smaller because we do all our reading in digital form, there might come a time when we barely have any paper books at home," says Bembibre. Should that day come, at least the scent of old books will have endured: grassy, sweet and steeped in a collective longing.

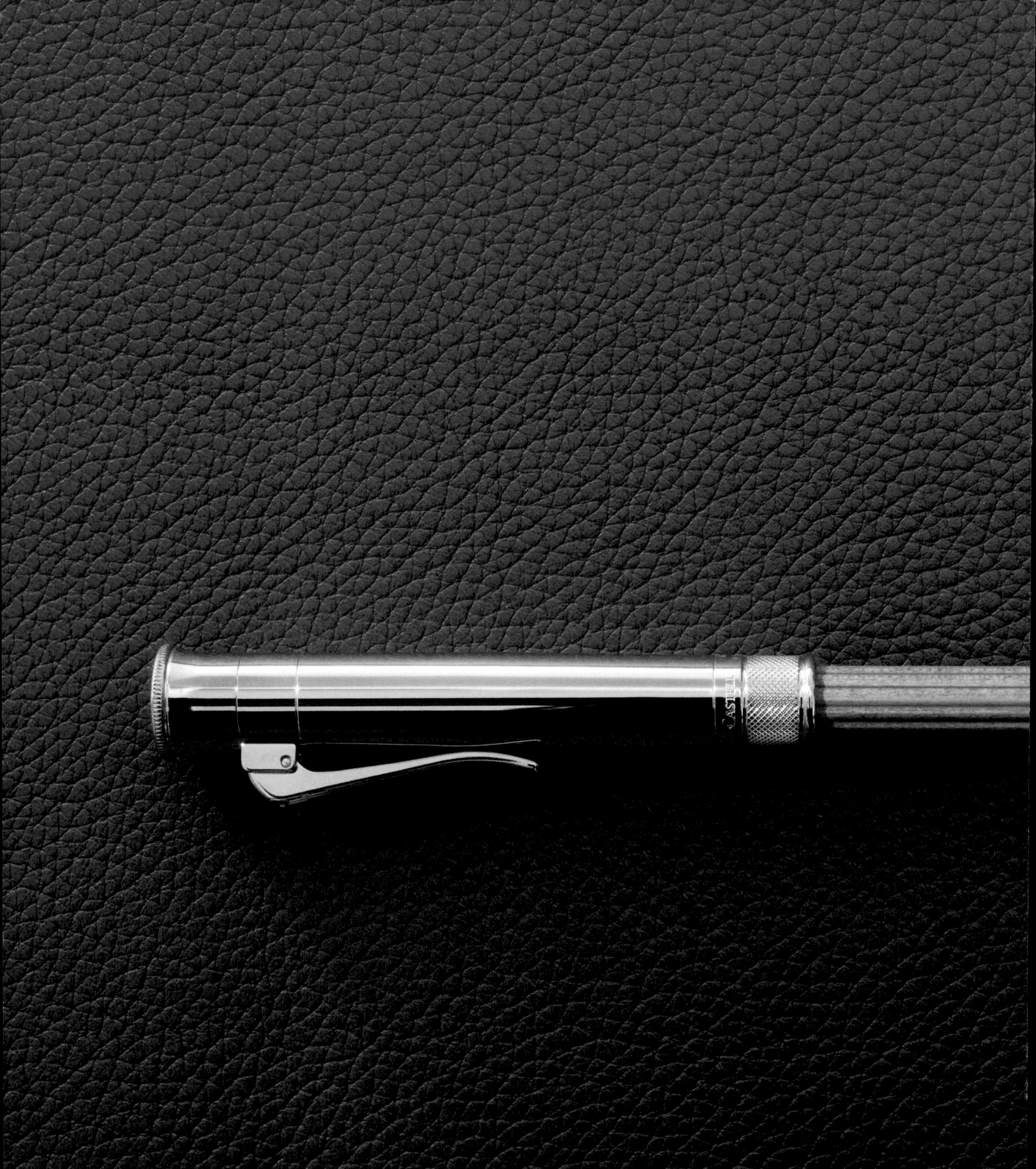

Answers by Jeremy Leslie

What's the correct way to read a magazine?
When people are browsing in our London shop they will pick up a magazine
and flick from the back, then flick from
the front, then stop at something in the
middle. The magazines I really enjoy I
will sit down with and try to avoid skim-
ming. I've made a lot of magazines and I
know the amount of care that goes into
the running order.

*Do you try to discourage visitors who browse
but never buy?* We're not like an old-fashioned newsagent who has a sticker on
every shelf saying "No browsing." Obviously, if someone browses for hours and
doesn't buy anything it's disappointing,
but for every person who does that, another
person will spend a few hours browsing
and then buy 20 magazines.

*Have magazines always been appreciated as
beautiful objects?* In the very beginning of
magazine publishing, the freesheets and
pamphlets that were distributed in cities
would have been very novel. It was only
at the end of the 20th century that we lost
sight of that, as magazines became com-
modities. Today, there's a renewed rele-
vance to the "object-ness" of magazines.
So, in a sense, we're returning to where we
came from.

*Are there aspects of historical magazine de-
sign you'd like to see resurrected?* There's a
gap between the traditional photocopied
fanzine type and the hugely "finished,"
matte paper independent magazines. I
think there's a really interesting point
between the two—something that uses
cheaper paper but still has great editorial intent and creativity behind it. I'd like
to see more ideas developed around that.

*Do you have a smart response when people
ask you if print is dead?* "Print is dead" is
dead. There was a time when it was a val-
id question, but we're over that now. We
have to move on.

Post Modern

Often, the thud of mail through the front door is met with a sigh. If it isn't an electricity bill, it's a once-in-a-lifetime promotion from a discount furniture store or a flyer from the local pizza place. The online world—with its minefield of political fearmongering, spam links and jealousy-inducing vacation photos from acquaintances—doesn't offer much more. Has the age of meaningful correspondence come to an end? And if so, what have we lost along the way?

The digital age has reformed both the way that we correspond and the means through which we can view others' correspondence. With letters, we are permitted unregulated access into the inner musings and fluctuating emotions of the author. And because of their sentimental sway they are usually lugged from one home to the next, all the great hopes and heartaches of a lifetime collected in a shoebox and stashed under the eaves. Emails, however, are password protected, guarded by privacy laws and unlikely to be found in an attic. Even if people did consciously donate their digital archives, these exchanges lack the same emotional resonance.

"Personally, I love receiving letters, especially now that it's so rare to get something through the post that isn't junk mail," says Simon Garfield, a British journalist and author of *To the Letter: A Celebra-* tion of the Lost Art of Letter Writing. Tracing the significance of letter writing throughout history—we have, he notes, relied upon it to communicate for more than 2,000 years—his book celebrates the legacy of numerous historical correspondences, like the unfolding (and then failing) relationship between Napoleon and his wife, Josephine. "As someone who writes a lot of history, I don't know where I'd be without archives and letters and the ability to track someone's life and transactions through the written word," he adds. "I don't think we've become less communicative," Garfield observes. "I just think the kind of depth and the lasting value of that communication through time has diminished."

Much of our reluctance toward letter writing boils down to convenience. The immediacy of email, and the omnipresence of social media, has made the delayed gratification of writing and waiting for a letter feel antiquated. Then there are the practicalities to contend with: a stamp to buy, the trip to a mailbox. But imagine hearing that thud through the mail slot and discovering a handwritten missive lying on the mat. Most likely it would be relished far more, and preserved much longer, than the email which arrives with a ping.

"We write letters in a different way than we compose emails and texts," Garfield continues. "They tend to take longer to compose, they tend to be better composed, and they have a beginning, middle and an end. We tend to dash off correspondence in a digital way far faster and with probably less imagination and perhaps more exactitude. They're great for business transactions, less so for emotional correspondence."

As letter writing falls by the wayside, Garfield has, ironically, found himself increasingly amenable to a form of correspondence usually met with derision: the annual Christmas letter. Long mocked by the likes of the late journalist Simon Hoggarts—who delighted so much in their bashing that he created *The Round Robin Letters*, an anthology compiling his favorites—the Christmas letter straddles an unusual fault line. Still a letter, but, like a Facebook status update, sent to a mass audience, it's a tradition imbued with bragging rights and blow-by-blow accounts of life's petty grievances. Yet even with their more distasteful aspects (Hoggart's book includes news of cats opening fridges and hamsters that love Puccini), Christmas letters represent a strain of personal letter writing that Garfield worries is fast becoming extinct. "I feel warmer towards those things because, along with condolence and thank-you notes, they may be one of the last bastions to fall," he says.

The Kinfolk Artwork Series

An exciting extension of *Kinfolk*'s ethos of fostering community and celebrating the many talents of our collaborators, *The Kinfolk Artwork Series* consists of three limited edition prints selected by the *Kinfolk* team.

Printed in Denmark on premium paper, each artwork is limited to a run of 250.

KINFOLK.COM/ARTWORK

4
Directory

Photograph: Marsý Hild Þórsdóttir

Elif Shafak

A conversation with Turkey's leading female author.

Writer Elif Shafak never takes the easy route. "World history shows we should be careful whenever anyone promises simple answers to complex questions," she says, speaking with characteristic precision. Whether teaching at the University of Oxford, lecturing on women's rights or writing one of the many novels and essays that have made her Turkey's most read female writer, she is an uncompromising public intellectual. Here, the *Honor* and *Three Daughters of Eve* author discusses what we can learn from belief systems that have been dismissed by many, her relationship with the Turkish and English languages and her penchant for goth metal music.

Why do you take issue with the idea of certainty? Life is closer to water than to stone. Humans learn a lot from opposites. For example, the conversation between faith and doubt is one that intrigues me a lot. People who cannot tolerate ambiguity can be present on both sides of this duality: Rigidly religious people want to get rid of doubt; rigid atheists want to get rid of faith. To me, they're doing the same thing—wanting to end the conversation. I personally feel closer to agnostic mystics, or "mysfits"—people who know that nothing is black and white.

You've often spoken fondly of your maternal grandmother, who was very traditional and religious. How has she influenced you? As a storyteller, I'm interested in how many women like her, in Turkey and around the world, were not allowed to pursue their education and yet at the same time strongly supported their daughters' and granddaughters' education. Also, they were often the bearers of collective memory; oral culture was transmitted from grandmothers to granddaughters. Especially in a country like Turkey, where there is systematic collective amnesia, it's incredibly important that these women carry this. The Western literary establishment does not always accept different kinds of storytelling though, looking down on them as less sophisticated. I sometimes hear judges in literary prizes saying, "This novel from Saudi Arabia or Indonesia is not how a novel should be written"—but there isn't only one formula. I've always been interested in bridging the gap between written and oral cultures.

Do you write differently in Turkish and English? Turkish is my grandmother and mother's tongue, the language of my childhood. It's very emotional. If I'm writing about melancholy, longing, sadness, I find it easier to do that in Turkish. With English, my relationship is much more cerebral. I feel a little more bold when I write in it because it frees me of cultural baggage. Humor, satire, irony is much easier for me in English.

Turkish, which is genderless and uses only one pronoun, is a completely different way of thinking. When people speak about God, for instance, there is no gender. The genderlessness allows the reader and the writer to use their imagination more, but it makes the task of translation quite difficult. We often talk about what is lost in translation, but many things are gained too. Many books are much better in their translated forms!

What part does silence play in your writing? In my work, I consistently attempt to give a voice to people who have been silenced, suppressed, forgotten and marginalized and bring them into the center. I remind the reader of their stories, making the invisible more visible. I want to be able to question taboos—political, sexual, cultural. A writer's job is to ask difficult questions about difficult issues, but not to provide answers. What matters is creating a free space where we can have a diversity of opinions and make the unspeakable speakable. But I find it very difficult to work in a silent environment, so I put on headphones and listen to very loud music on repeat.

People must be taken aback by your taste in music, for example your love of Scandinavian metal bands. What attracts you to this music? I've always liked industrial, symphonic and goth metal because it's very much about opposites: compassion and criticism, light and a lot of darkness. That high energy is very important to my writing. People are surprised when they hear my taste. When I love a song, I have to listen to it on repeat—sometimes 90 times while I'm writing. The loop, circles within circles, helps me to concentrate.

"There is a silent wisdom in the oral tradition which is mostly appreciated by women in countries such as mine," says Shafak, who believes that the Western literary establishment has a close-minded understanding of what counts as great writing.

Daniel Mallory Ortberg, author of *The Merry Spinster*, praises the caustic wit of mid-century novelist *Barbara Pym*.

DANIEL MALLORY ORTBERG

Peer Review

Pym's subtle observational style fell out of favor during the hedonistic 1960s, but her reputation has been advancing steadily ever since—so much so that "Pymish" is now used as a metaphor for brittle, delicately humorous writing.

It was Carrie Frye, former managing editor of idiosyncratic news website *The Awl* who set my feet on the path of righteousness when she described Barbara Pym's work as "spinster drag novels" and instructed me to hold off on *Crampton Hodnet* until after I'd taken a crack at *Excellent Women*. I'd had a vague sense of Pym's oeuvre before that, of course—I could conjure up dim pictures of a mid-century British woman standing in front of a kitchen sink, a resentful curate, the feeling of going out to buy a new dress and feeling disproportionately hopeless about the entire human condition as a result—but it wasn't until Frye described the compensatory pleasures of the pose of unrequited love "narratively severed from its object" that I really started to pay attention. In an unpublished early novel, Pym writes: "She had been in love with [him] for so long that she could not imagine a life in which he had no part. Nor, on the other hand, could she imagine a life in which he returned her love. That would somehow spoil the picture she had made of herself, it was an interesting picture, very dear to her, and she could not bear the idea of it being spoilt." Pym is a connoisseur of the drawn-out social humiliation, but her books somehow make one bloom rather than cringe in sympathetic embarrassment and self-recrimination—one responds by opening up, rather than shrinking inward, in reading about the sort of situation one ordinarily would do anything to avoid.

The comparisons to Austen are numerous and, at this point, mandatory, so let's get them out of the way as quickly as possible: They're both meticulously observant, acutely aware of social niceties and social disaster, interested in the inner lives of women, and rather inclined to laugh at their own tendencies toward melancholy. But Pym deserves more than the perfunctory, algorithmic, "if-you-liked-Austen-you'll-like-these-similar-titles" recommendation. She's the master of the 20th-century, middle-class, heterosexual case study, an affectionate but clear-eyed examiner of masculine self-seriousness. From *Crampton Hodnet* (which I successfully held off on reading until I'd finished *Excellent Women* and *Less Than Angels*): "What city in the world was more romantic than Paris, provided one didn't lose one's luggage?" Pym never forgets the luggage.

Left Photographs: See Credits on page 191, Right Photograph: Aaron Tilley

PAPER CLIP APOCALYPSE
by Harriet Fitch Little

While loved by designers, the paper clip has far fewer positive associations for researchers of artificial intelligence. The paper clip maximizer theory—a canonical thought experiment used to illustrate the possibility of a robot apocalypse—imagines a scenario in which an algorithm is tasked with the seemingly mundane responsibility of amassing paper clips. At first it gathers boxes from shops, then pulls them off documents, then—ultimately—builds paper clip factories and begins tearing down steel-supported buildings in order to feed its insatiable, preprogrammed appetite. The conclusion: Even the most banal use of AI can turn nasty, and quick. (Top: Oversized paper clip by Carl Auböck, Center: Classic brass paper clips by Present & Correct, Bottom: Clip Clip in brass by HAY.)

Object Matters

A short history of the paper clip.

Designers can be devilish contrarians. In *Century Makers*—a 1998 book about the 20th century's most life-changing innovations—David Hillman and David Gibbs praise the paper clip: an object so small and mundane that one would think it unlikely to quicken the pulses of even the most obsessive stationery nerds. But the Davids are not alone in their love of this run-of-the-mill filing aid. In 2004 it sat behind glass in New York's Museum of Modern Art, as part of their *Humble Masterpieces* exhibition.

Why has a simple piece of double-looped bent wire been imbued with such celebrity? To understand, it is worth considering some history. In the 19th century, the industrial revolution spread across the globe and commerce boomed. But with progress came paperwork—mounds of letters, invoices and receipts. In 1899, a Norwegian patent clerk named Johan Vaaler patented a paper clip design formed of a single wire loop, feeding into the myth that Vaaler was the "inventor" of the now-ubiquitous two-loop clip. In fact, the familiar double loop design known then, as now, as the "Gem," was already in wide circulation in Vaaler's time—although presumably not in Norway—alongside a diverse array of competing clip shapes.

What is clear from inspection of these early competing designs is that the Gem has an obvious edge. It occupies a sweet spot in terms of the necessary compromises between function, form and ease of manufacture; other clips use more steel or more complex forms, or feature protruding ends more likely to snag paper.

When paper files made way for computerized ones, the Gem followed: Early users of Microsoft Office were offered advice (often unsolicited) by a virtual assistant called Clippit—an anthropomorphic paper clip with googly eyes who has retained cult status as a social media meme. Clippit was retired in 2007. Yet even in his absence, and despite the dwindling of paper bureaucracy, designers still love the paper clip. Why? Perhaps because it has achieved something that few man-made objects ever do: In an industry driven by the desire to reinvent or at least endlessly tweak functionality, it has proved itself un-improvable.

Cult Rooms

Built like a boat, a Kew Gardens greenhouse where marooned palms flourish.

The Palm House at London's Kew Gardens, completed in 1848, looks like a steamship plowing through a sea of green. The metaphor is apt because the explorers of that era would compete by sailing home from foreign travels with the most bizarre species they could find and bringing them to Kew. One highlight, for example, is the Madagascan suicide palm, which flowers once in 50 years then promptly expires. The Palm House's oldest plant, an *Encephalartos altensteinii* palm, was picked up in the 1770s during Captain Cook's second circumnavigation.

It's not that the Palm House architects were trying to conjure nautical imagery. But as no one had built a greenhouse of its size before, draftsmen looked for stability in ship design, with its stress-absorbing lines and spilling tiers. In a neat coincidence, architects would go on to equate the gathering age of steam with modernity. Le Corbusier, who traveled on steamships for commissions in São Paulo and New York, labeled them "a liberation from the cursed enslavement of the past." Ships were passports to a more fabulous age. The trick for the Kew architects was to distill shipbuilding style into the world's largest greenhouse. For this they turned to two bewhiskered Victorian greats. The first was all-around ironman Richard Turner—a fellow so obsessed with the material that he pioneered the creation of railway buildings, cisterns and bedsteads in wrought iron. The second was the impossibly well-connected designer Decimus Burton. Not only was he the 10th child of Georgian

London's top property developer, Burton was also a founding fellow of the Royal Institute of British Architects and an early member of the Athenaeum, the Pall Mall club that he himself designed at the tender age of 24.

Turner had recently constructed the vast Palm House in Belfast, a few miles from where the Titanic was later built. This was a time when Britain felt flush with the trappings of a golden industrial age. The Victorians created, among other things, the pedal bicycle, photography, postage stamps, post boxes, Easter eggs and the typewriter. The SS Great Britain, the world's first ironclad transatlantic steamship, would soon set sail for New York.

Burton, ever the conceptualizer, proposed the idea of a floating two-tiered sweeping structure for Kew. It would be curvilinear—Sydney Opera-esque. Turner, the more down-to-earth of the pair, declared they would do the lot in wrought iron, arguing that his iron arch ribs, originally designed for ship decks, would allow the roof to reach 50 feet between the supporting columns, creating a sunlit wonderland below. As the structure towered up to 65 feet, a veritable jungle could be planted within. There was room for ducts, vents and steam radiators to maintain a tropical fug. And there was to be a spiraling staircase (made of iron, naturally) that led up to an ornately banistered treetop walkway.

The end result was swooshy and voluptuous. The final effect is a cathedral of plants, and a temple to the Victorian can-do spirit. In fact, it performed its role as

a hothouse so successfully that some plants were burned alive during the first year. A decade later Kew asked Burton to return. In 1860, he designed the Temperate House to accommodate floral curiosities from Britain's expanding colonies in Australasia, Polynesia and Asia. It was twice the size of the Palm House, and it became the largest greenhouse in the world.

A few 21st-century accoutrements have since been added on to the Palm House. Atomized humidification maintains a condensation that melts the face like a hard night in New Orleans. And no-rust paint keeps the baroque balustrades from crumbling—even in a climate that can sustain the *Elaeis guineensis* oil palm, which is as happy here as it is back in Equatorial Guinea. As the world's most noted botanist, Sir David Attenborough, states: "Rainforests occupy only two percent of the world's land surface but they contain over 50 percent of the world's species. To study them, Kew has built a rainforest on the banks of the River Thames." For all its modernity, both ancient and recent, keeping the 16,000 panes shipshape still requires old-fashioned elbow grease. Manual window cleaning takes place once a decade and can last up to two months.

The epicenter of the Palm House is adorned with a final apt symbol: A sculpture depicts Hercules wrestling the river god Achelous, a battle that Hercules won. To some, it represents the taming of Mother Nature by the swinging thrust of modern man. Fortunately, Kew has preserved a lost world for all to see.

Eleven years after Burton completed The Palm House, he began work on a new building at Kew Gardens that would dwarf it. The Temperate House was twice the size, and so flamboyant that one politican complained to parliament that Kew risked becoming a "gaudy flower garden."

CHARLES SHAFAIEH

Rock the Cradle

Lullabies have the sedative power to soothe — and to scare.

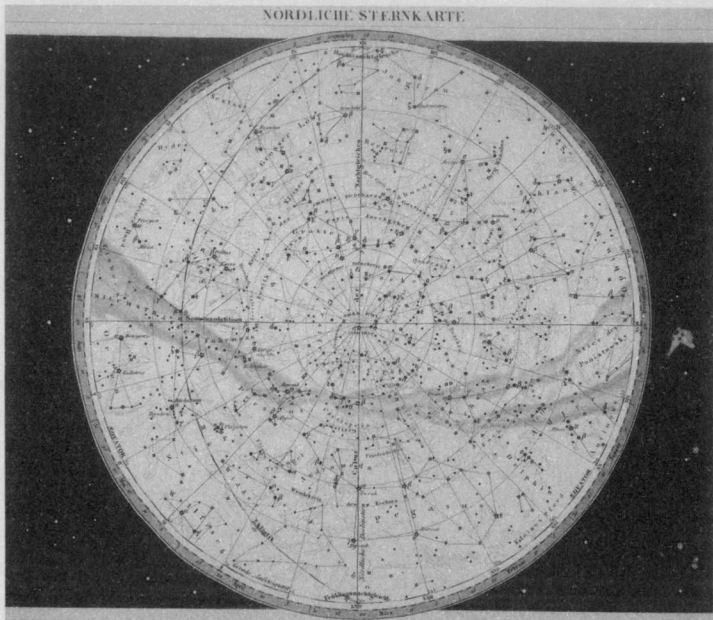

NORDLICHE STERNKARTE

Lullabies are often at the center of the most intimate moments between a child and their loved ones. A private space forms around singer and audience—a kind of temporary, invisible womb—in which begins what Spanish playwright Federico García Lorca called "a little initiation into poetic adventure." Like magical incantations, these typically slow tunes, limited in melodic range, are transformative. As Lorca put it: "The mother transports the child beyond himself, into the remote distance, and returns him weary to her lap, to rest."

Paradoxically, the lullaby is a uniquely adult genre. The musical simplicity allows for textual inventiveness, and it is a blessing, in many ways, that children cannot understand the words—as the lyrics often would do little to soothe young minds. In Japan, for example, traditional *Itsuki* lullabies served as a pressure valve for poor teenage girls employed as live-in nannies, who could sing of their despair and traumas without fear of censure. Russian women have experienced the same release, with their East Slavic lullabies often concerning wicked husbands.

Some spiritual traditions impose strict rules on who can perform certain lullabies, and for which audiences. Many unmarried Italian women would not sing them, ethnomusicologist Alan Lomax discovered in the 1950s, because childbearing was intimately associated with the act of sex. For the Yanyuwa people in Australia, numerous lullabies are said to have originated during the mythological period of prehistory known as the Dreamtime. "They tell us about the country. They are maps which we carry in our heads," Mussolini Harvey, a Yanyuwa man, has explained. "Some of these songs are dangerous, they are secret and sacred. This is why many are exclusively meant for, or sung by, only one sex."

Often simultaneously tender and terrifying, both of the present and tied to ancient traditions, lullabies help form our sense of self and also embed cultural memories within us. Composer and performer Sophia Brous says she learned this in her research for her song cycle *Lullaby Movement*. "Prompting a connection to these melodies was like connecting to a person's essence and essential being, taking them back to deeply intimate, loving, but sometimes also painful memories," she says. "The vulnerability that a child feels at the edge of sleep, and the salve of the voice that is comforting and calling as night drifts in, remains with us forever."

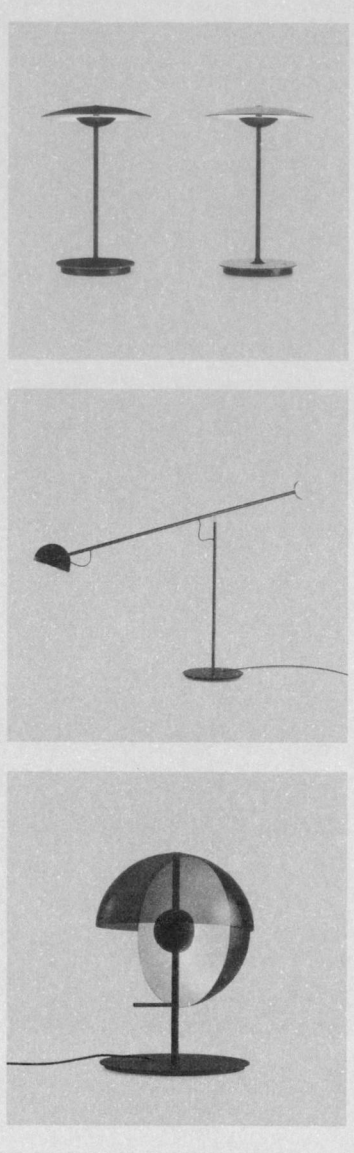

OUT LIKE A LIGHT
by Harriet Fitch Little

Poltergeists have long been associated with flickering bulbs. Mediums believe that it's a friendly way that ghosts have of reminding the living of their presence, while more hardheaded ghost hunters think the dimming of bulbs is the result of spirits using electricity as energy. Like the twilight zone, there's something about the liminal state of a flickering bedside light that strikes our suggestible minds as mysterious. In his poem *Locksley Hall*, Alfred, Lord Tennyson sets the scene for an occult encounter. The spirit will come, he says, "Where the dying night-lamp flickers, and the shadows rise and fall." Perhaps it's the supernatural making itself known. Perhaps it's that old houses—the ones that feel so spooky—often just have faulty wiring. Either way, best to keep a spare bulb in your bedside table. (Top: Ginger Portable Lamp by Joan Gaspar, Center: Copérnica Lamp by Ramírez i Carrillo, Bottom: Theia Lamp by Mathias Hahn. All by Marset Lamps.)

Left Photograph: Bettmann/Getty Images, Right Photographs: Courtesy of Marset Lamps

Human hibernation is the stuff of fairytales.
Is it also the key to space travel?

Photograph: Peter Purdy/BIPs/Getty Images

ALEX ANDERSON

Stay Woke

Doctors sometimes induce a form of
short-term hibernation in patients;
during brain surgery they may cool the
body for up to an hour in order to stop
blood circulating.

As winter approaches and thoughts turn to the dark, frigid days ahead, we may fantasize about hiding somewhere and waking with the crocuses in March. Hedgehogs, ground squirrels and bears do it—bedding down for months in musky burrows. Hibernation sounds appealing, but aside from the obvious benefits of not having to arrive at work before sunrise and dodging snow-shoveling duties, it would not be very pleasant. During hibernation, core temperature drops, systems slow and the body gradually exhausts itself—hardly a restful way to pass the season.

The human hibernation of popular culture misses this point entirely. In the Brothers Grimm version of *Sleeping Beauty*, the princess wakes fresh-faced and cheerful after a hundred years of slumber. Rip Van Winkle stirs from his 20-year snooze, in Washington Irving's 19th-century yarn, with a stretch and a nose for breakfast. More recent fiction presents human hibernation slightly more realistically—and unpleasantly—in long-distance space travel. In *2001: A Space Odyssey* three scientists heading to Jupiter lie sealed in white sarcophagi, only to perish as the malevolent shipboard computer shuts down their life support. Space travelers in *Passengers* and *Interstellar* lie insensate in similar hibernation pods, prepared to emerge as the curve of some distant planet fills the portholes.

Yet in reality, human hibernation would probably look more like the torpor of ground squirrels than the technological entombment of space fiction. Claude Piantadosi, an expert on space survival, points out that a major aim of inducing hibernation would be to reduce cargo. Having astronauts fuel up before leaving would achieve this most efficiently. A hibernating traveler outbound to Mars would metabolize only 8½ pounds of stored fat during the seven-month journey, saving 550 pounds in food, water and oxygen. But like any other hibernating mammal, an astronaut would need to move around occasionally to prevent atrophy of muscles, bones and brain. Space sarcophagi would hinder both of these goals: not only are they heavy, they severely inhibit movement. Comfortable, well-monitored berths would serve the hibernating traveler better.

However it happens for enchanted princesses or space travelers, we humans aren't going to sleep through the winter. So we'll get up early and we'll shovel the snow, but we'll also need to find ways to enjoy the dark and the cold.

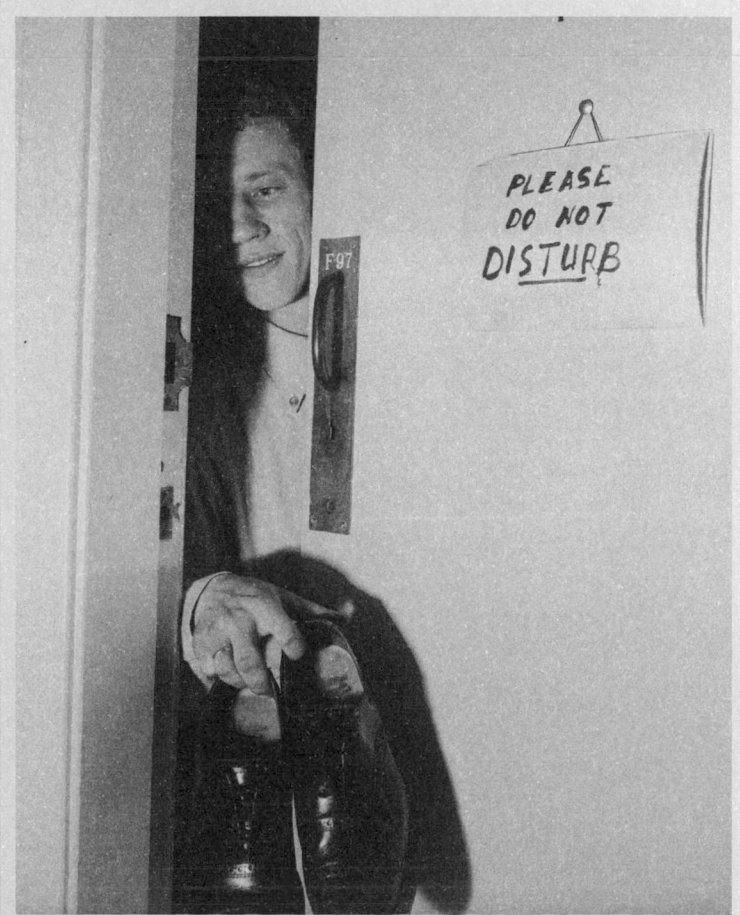

The small print: decipher starred clues by tearing away the word "paper."

MOLLY YOUNG

Crossword

ACROSS

1. *Softcover book
5. Bucatini or penne
10. *The New York Times or Le Monde
14. Water, en español
15. 1979 Ridley Scott film starring Sigourney Weaver
16. Leave out
17. Ogle
18. Disco queen Summer
19. Non-edible morsel you might add to soup for extra flavor
20. Literary form popularized by Montaigne
22. Number of Commandments in the Old Testament
23. Entry on an agenda
24. Asian New Year
26. Like most internet access
29. Cheddar and Gruyère
33. Somewhat
34. ___ Vegas
35. Letters before an alias
37. Bandit
41. Rapscallions
43. Add to the starred clues (either at the front or the back) to solve
45. Spiritual practice from India
46. Hitchcock film with an infamous shower scene
48. Wee bit
49. Nourished
50. Blamed for Black Death
52. Tells
55. Evaluated
59. Whistle blower in sport
60. Pal
61. Quarrel
63. Sketched
67. "Agreed!"
68. Party souvenir
70. Twin brother of Jacob
71. Annoyed
72. Madama Butterfly or Tosca
73. Where you set a pie to cool
74. *Woodworker's smoothing aid
75. Upbeat
76. Edvard Grieg's In the ___ of the Mountain King

DOWN

1. Unit of hay
2. Grows older
3. Stage directions
4. Japanese martial art
5. ___ thai (noodle dish)
6. "Thanks ___!"
7. Tendon
8. Sport that can be played on grass, clay or hardcourt
9. California's Santa ___ winds
10. Aristocracy
11. Overact, theatrically
12. Sommelier's offerings
13. Flower stalks
21. Influential English prog rock band
25. Vessels for steeped beverages
27. Stock up again
28. World's second largest bird (after the ostrich)
29. *Fastener used in an office
30. Sandwich meats
31. Observe
32. Music genre that is a forerunner to rocksteady
36. Suitable
38. Artist's place
39. James who wrote The Night of the Hunter screenplay
40. Large quantities
42. Showed, as a movie
44. Site of Vincent Van Gogh's famous injury
47. Owns
51. Vibrant shawl of Mexican origin
53. Showed the way
54. All over again
55. Store up
56. Island located between Hawaii and New Zealand
57. Unyielding
58. White-cliffed port on the English coastline
62. *Tax forms and such
64. Tibet's continent
65. *Patterned room decoration
66. Nonexistent
68. Dandy
69. Davies of The Kinks

You can't judge a book by its cover, or a gift by the quality of its wrapping. Yet studies have shown exactly that: An artfully finished piece of packaging influences our perception of the quality of the item it contains. For *Kinfolk*, design writer and *Pretty Packages* author *Sally Shim* explains how to use paper and scissors (but never single-sided tape) to add a final flourish to your gifts.

Some people believe more is better, but I believe less is more. I'm not a fan of store-bought wrapping paper and poly star gift bows. I also steer clear of gift wrap sets that include matching wrap, ribbon and tag. My approach is minimalist: Start with a base of kraft paper or white butcher paper, then create embellishments that add texture and interesting details, such as a yarn pom-pom or a polymer clay gift tag. When designing your wrapping, consider the culturally specific symbolism behind colors. In Western cultures, red is bold, orange is fun, yellow is cheerful. In Japan, red symbolizes life and vitality, orange is love and happiness and yellow is beauty and courage. Japan has some of the most beautifully wrapped gifts in the world, involving precise folds and intricate pleats. Italians are also ones to watch: They're known for their luxurious decorative papers, like hand-marbled paper.

There are three key components in creating beautifully wrapped gifts: Invest in quality materials and tools; learn how to wrap packages with perfectly creased edges (hint: use a bone folder) and always use double-sided tape so the packages are free from translucent tape. Although professionally wrapped gifts are fine, don't underestimate the beauty of hand wrapping. More than the visual appeal, the sentiment behind it is priceless.

FOLK 'N' ROLL

AW 18/19

WOLF&RITA

Stockists

3.1 PHILLIP LIM
31philliplim.com

ALESSI
alessi.com

ANDERSON & SHEPPARD
anderson-sheppard.co.uk

ARJOWIGGINS
arjowigginscreativepapers.com

ARMOR LUX
armorlux.com

CÉLINE
celine.com

COS
cosstores.com

DEVEAUX
deveauxnewyork.com

DRIES VAN NOTEN
driesvannoten.be

ERIK JORGENSEN
erik-joergensen.com

EUDON CHOI
eudonchoi.com

FILIPPA K
filippa-k.com

FIORELLA PRATTO
fiorellapratto.com

GRAF VON FABER-CASTELL
graf-von-faber-castell.com

HANDVAERK
handvaerk.com

HANIEL JEWELRY
hanieljewelry.com

HAY
hay.dk

HERMÈS
hermes.com

J.W. ANDERSON
j-w-anderson.com

JOHN LOBB
johnlobb.com

LAURENCE AIRLINE
laurenceairline.com

LELLOUE
lelloue.com

LEVI'S
levi.com

LINDBERG
lindberg.com

LOSTINE
lostine.com

MACKINTOSH
mackintosh.com

MADS NØRGAARD
madsnorgaard.com

MAISON MARGIELA
maisonmargiela.com

MALENE BIRGER
bymalenebirger.com

MARGARET HOWELL
margarethowell.co.uk

MARNI
marni.com

MARSET
marset.com

MILLIGRAM
milligram.com

MULBERRY
mulberry.com

MYKITA
mykita.com

NK FINE WRITING
nk.se

ODE TO THINGS
odetothings.com

PARACHUTE HOME
parachutehome.com

PAUL SMITH
paulsmith.com

PAUSTIAN
paustian.com

PRESENT & CORRECT
presentandcorrect.com

PRINGLE OF SCOTLAND
pringlescotland.com

RAINS
rains.com

RED WING
redwingshoes.com

RYAN LO
ryanlo.co.uk

SADAK
sadak.de

SAND COPENHAGEN
sandcopenhagen.com

SANDRO
sandro-paris.com

SLOWEAR
slowear.com

SOLOVIÈRE
soloviere.com

SONIA RYKIEL
soniarykiel.com

STRING
string.se

THE JOURNAL SHOP
thejournalshop.com

THEORY
theory.com

TIBI
tibi.com

TINA FREY
tinafreydesigns.com

TOTÊME
toteme-studio.com

TOTOKAELO
totokaelo.com

VIVIENNE WESTWOOD
viviennewestwood.com

WOLF & RITA
wolfandrita.com

ISSUE 29

Credits

COVER
Photographer
Pelle Crépin
Stylist
David Nolan
Hair Stylist
Antonio De Luca using
Bumble & Bumble
Makeup Artist
Teddy Mitchell using Bobbi
Brown
Assistants
Benjamin Whitley
Joseph Seresin
Model
Xiaomeng Huang
Casting
Sarah Bunter
Coat by Mulberry and
earrings by COS

P. 22
Art Director
Dominic Webster
Stylist
Nicque Patterson
Shoes by Purified Footwear

P. 26
Louis wears trousers by
Laurence Airline, a trench
by Sadak, shoes by Solovière
and sunglasses by Scene
Number For

P. 28
Photograph:
Alamy Stock Photo

P. 36
Pepper Mills: Photographs
courtesy of Lostine, Wall-
paper*STORE and Alessi

P. 44
Anh wears a top by COS

P. 46
Pullover by 3.1 Phillip Lim

P. 47
Tuxedo jacket by Tibi

P. 48
Sweater by Sunspel

P. 75
Shirin wears a gown
by 3.1 Phillip Lim

P. 84 - 95
Hair Stylist
Kirstine Engell
Makeup Artist
Stine Rasmussen
Models
Adrian Bosch
Thula Neka
Casting
Sarah Bunter

P. 96 - 105
Assistants
Patrick Molina
Mark Underwood

P. 120 - 129
Hair Stylist
Antonio De Luca
using Bumble &
Bumble
Makeup Artist
Teddy Mitchell using
Bobbi Brown
Assistants
Benjamin Whitley
Joseph Seresin
Models
Xiaomeng Huang
Reuben Chapman
Casting
Sarah Bunter

P. 120
Kaftan by Lelloue,
socks and earrings by
COS and shoes by
John Lobb

P. 121
Coat by Mulberry and
earrings by COS

P. 134 & 137
André wears turtlenecks
by Theory

P. 142
Shirt by COS, trousers
by Marni and *André's*
own jacket

P. 148
Calligraphy Tools:
Photographs courtesy
of Milligram, *Christian
Møller Andersen* and The
Journal Shop

P. 160 - 163
This article is an abridged
and edited excerpt from
Bookshelf (Object Lessons,
Bloomsbury Academic,
2016) republished with
the kind permission of
its author Lydia Pyne and
Bloomsbury Academic

P. 164 - 175
Hand Model
Anastasia / Röster
Grooming
Lovisa Lunneborg
Assistant
Per Nilsson
Retouching
Matilda / La Machine
Agency
LundLund

P. 172 - 173
Pencil: Graf von Faber-
Castell, Desk Mat: Perfect
Pencil Platina by Ramos
from NK Fine Writing

P. 181
Paper Clips: Photographs
courtesy of Ode to Things,
Present & Correct and
Christian Møller Andersen

P. 182 - 183
Photograph: Charles
Chusseau-Flaviens/George
Eastman Museum/Getty
Images

Special Thanks:
Barbara Pym Society
Julian Lloyd & London
Library
Molly Mandell
Niels Strøyer
Christophersen
Paustian

Frame: MYKITA LITE ELVE | Photography: Mark Borthwick